LIFE OF A SALESMAN

RUPERT HARRY MILLER

 Published by Rupert Miller.

Cover design by Spiffing Covers Ltd

Paperback ISBN – 978-1-910256-88-6
.epub ISBN – 978-1-910256-89-3
.mobi ISBN – 978-1-910256-90-9

Dedicated to Julian David Miller

3rd November 1962 - 6th December 1991

"It is amazing what you can accomplish if you do not care who gets the credit."
Harry S. Truman

Chapter One

"Rupert! Why are your trouser pockets stuffed full of money?"

At that very instant I knew my highly lucrative *business empire* would collapse.

Why hadn't I emptied my pockets before my mother found them in the laundry basket? God only knows, but I didn't, and now I'd have to 'incur the displeasure of the Army Board', in other words, face my father. Had I been older, the presence of all that cash in my pockets could have been explained away by a visit to a machine, but it was 1965 and I was only seven years old. I was in a pickle, the first of many.

Baycliffe School had closed down so I was sent to Netherton House; I was still too young to join my brother at prep school. Baycliffe was a small school with no tuck shop and Netherton House was a vast school with a huge tuck shop. We lived in a bloody big house in Cheshire since my father was the Chairman and Managing Director of a company that manufactured shirts for M&S. He made loads of money and could afford staff. We had a cook, two housemaids and a gardener. However, unlike the Ferrantis, who lived in Knutsford, we had no butler. This infuriated my mother.

You see, because we had a cook, pocket money was superfluous to requirements. Mrs Shufflebottom, or 'Shuffy' as she was known, was an excellent pastry chef and made little biscuits and other tasty morsels for me to take to school in lieu of the far more glamorous collection of confectionary that was on sale in the Netherton House school tuck shop. While her pseudo-tuck was delicious, it did nothing for my street credibility at school. In fact, it became a source of financial embarrassment, as all my peers had cash for tuck and I had none. At break I used to sit on my own munching one of Shuffy's oatmeal shortcakes and watch my 'friends' suck on their Sherbet Fountains and chew Mars bars. It was just not fair. Somehow I had to devise a way of getting some cash quickly.

To just tell Mrs Shufflebottom that her services were no longer needed because I had found another tuck sponsor would be out of the question. She ruled the roost. Shuffy was about four foot two in every direction. She behaved exactly like Mrs. Patmore in *Downton Abbey* and we ate what she put on the table with no argument. This never posed a problem as her cooking was excellent. All the vegetables were grown in the walled garden by our gardener, Charlie, who also happened to be Mr. Shufflebottom. He was tiny too, but unlike his wife, he was as thin as a rake.

Diminutive as he was, he was still very much in charge of the garden as my father found out early on in his tenure as the new owner of 'The Pole'. One season he felt that we had a little too much cauliflower and not enough carrots. This was mentioned to Charlie in passing and the next year we got nothing but carrots.

The Pole was a very pretty Georgian mansion set in three acres of lawns and woodland. Next to the large walled garden was a stable block that had been converted into servants' quarters at the turn of the century. The main house had six bedrooms, three bathrooms, a nursery, a very large kitchen, a cosy sitting room, a cloak room, a gun room, an extensive wine cellar, a grand dining room and a very beautiful and formal drawing room for sipping sherry prior to the Sunday roast.

When my father found the house in 1953 it was in a bit of a state as it had not been lived in since before the Second World War. It was on the market for the sum of five thousand pounds and he was able to buy it as, apart from inheriting the family textile business from his father in 1942, he had also received a nice cash sum. In 1954 he moved in with two friends, Fergus Pope and an Austrian Count called Ervine Gitschmann-Valdick who was definitely the 'only gay in the village'.

During the house renovation, they camped in the kitchen; the only water supply coming from a lead pipe which they had to open and close with a pair of pliers.

My father was an excellent tennis player, and some say that if it hadn't been for the War he would have played at Wimbledon. After work and before returning to The Pole for dinner, the three friends would often meet up at the local tennis club for a few sets of mixed doubles. Mixed doubles meant girls and, although Ervine did not know one end of a girl from the other, after one of these tournaments he sidled up to my father and said,

"David I have just seen your future wife."

Well, my father told him not to be so stupid but Ervine insisted that he should at least meet this young lady. My father eventually agreed and Ervine arranged a game of mixed doubles for the next weekend. My father's partner for the game was the very beautiful, twenty-two year old daughter of Harry and Edith Prestt, Christine Ann, but known only as 'Ann'. Harry Prestt was a successful cotton broker in Liverpool and Manchester and they lived in a large house just outside Wigan, Lancashire. Ann having attended the Ladies Finishing School, Winkfield near Ascot had been a debutante in London, going to all the fancy Balls during the 'Season'. She had appeared in *Tatler* on many occasions and once was on the front page of the *Daily Express*. Ann was much admired and had many suitors.

At the end of the tennis match, which my father and Ann won easily, he thought that she was a spoilt brat and far too pretty for her own good. She thought that he was an arrogant sod who was far too good at tennis for his own good. They parted company with a polite, but curt handshake.

Ervine was not convinced, so decided to take matters further. He went to the car park while Ann and my father were avoiding each other in the tea rooms. He took Ann's tennis racket out of the boot of her car and put it in the boot of my father's car. He then put my father's racket into the boot of Ann's car. Ervine was easily able to do this as in those days nobody locked anything.

When my father got home he noticed that his racket seemed to have shrunk and then he spotted the name, ANN PRESTT, stenciled down one side of the racket handle. He traced her number through The Northern Club and Ann and my father agreed to meet the following day to exchange tennis rackets. Three months later they married.

They did not hang about. Clunie arrived almost without delay, I arrived not much later and had it not been for a miscarriage, Julian would have made it three in four years. My mother wanted a cricket team but father had to continually remind her that children were very expensive and the number of cheques left in her cheque book had no correlation whatsoever with the state of their bank balance.

And speaking of money, I needed to generate some in order to fund my tuck cravings. Stealing it was out of the question so I had to come up with either a product or a service that others would want. My first idea, www.rubbers.com, involved unscrewing the rubber stoppers from the bottom of school chairs and offering them at discounted prices or on a 'buy-one-get-one-free' basis to my unsuspecting classroom colleagues.

Business was brisk but two problems arose: firstly, there was a limited supply of this natural resource and, secondly, the chairs now made a hell of a noise when moved. Apart from being brisk this business was also short-lived but it did give me the confidence to embark upon www.taketheblame.com. This turned out to be less labour intensive than www.rubbers.com and far more lucrative.

Taketheblame Ltd. worked liked this. For a small fee, I would agree to 'own up' to any minor crime such as smashing a window or scribbling on a school textbook. As a result, I quickly became the naughtiest boy in the school by a country mile. And despite the fact that I appeared to be in two totally different places at the same time, it did not raise any suspicions for a remarkably long time. Fortunately, my punishments were not financial so I kept the fees.

My third and most daring money-making enterprise was www.georgieporgiepuddingandpie.com. As the website address suggests, this involved kissing and girls. It was without doubt the most unpleasant of activities but, as we say up North, "Where there's muck, there's brass!" My male customers were quite happy to pay a premium to watch me run up to a girl and give her a kiss. None of this snogging stuff, as it was clearly stated in the contract that a simple peck on the cheek would satisfy my obligations. Despite the utterly revolting nature of the work involved, I somehow managed to force myself every day to do it to ensure that I kept the cash rolling in. The only bonus in this business was that the girls did not seem to mind and I was never reported.

So I now found myself with plenty of money for tuck. Mission accomplished. In fact, I had too much money. I used the surplus funds to purchase extra tuck which I gave away. As well as now being the naughtiest boy in the school, I had rapidly become one of the most popular and really felt that life just could not possibly be any sweeter. Being in such a position and only seven years old, I felt like one of the 'Untouchables' but, as we all know, they came to a very sticky end. I wonder how long my devilish empire would have lasted had my mother not found the money in my trousers? The Fraud Squad moved in quickly, the evidence was gathered and after a short meeting between my parents and the school, I was duly expelled.

My expulsion came close to the end of the school term and, as I was nearly eight, my father persuaded the Dragon School in Oxford to take me a term early. In addition, he also gave me pocket money to discourage further business ventures.

Unlike Netherton House, the Dragon School was a boarding school and we were closely monitored at all times. There was a tuck shop but as I had ample legitimate funds, there was no need to get creative. The closest I got to wheeling and dealing was with marbles and conkers, but these did not have the same allure as hard cash and there was no risk involved. It was all pretty mundane. Just for fun and a little bonus I thought about resurrecting www.georgieporgiepuddingandpie.com, but as the only girls in the school were the offspring of teachers and, as such, few in number, this idea was swiftly shelved. It would have been far too dangerous anyway, and the idea of kissing girls as a pleasant experience was some way off.

So at the Dragon School I did not sell one single thing. In fact, the only real spice in my life was trying to avoid being caught smoking. Ironically I was finally nabbed by my key-throwing Latin master whose own addiction to nicotine was so rampant he could have captained the Portuguese National Smoking Team. 'Putty', as he was nicknamed, needed to nip out of the classroom during lessons to get his fix. The slimy red faced bastard reported me and I got whacked.

Harrow, or the 'Dump on the Hump' as it was affectionately known, was to be my next stop. Lord Byron, Winston Churchill and Jawaharlal Nehru all attended this prestigious establishment in North West London, but despite the achievement of these three, Harrow did not immediately provide any opening for a budding salesman. It was not until I had been there for nearly four years that an opportunity presented itself.

Harrow was also a boarding school and made up of several houses with approximately one hundred boys per house. Each house had a hierarchy which consisted of: House Monitors at the top, Four Yearers, Three Yearers, Two Yearers and the rest. The House Master and his wife were in charge but much of the day-to-day running of the house, such as organising house sports teams, was left up to the boys.

Although mobile phones did not exist, Harrow had a very good, albeit primitive way of communicating: the 'Fag' system. On arrival at the school each new boy would become the personal slave of the House Monitors for his first two terms. This involved cleaning shoes, making beds and running errands. If a Monitor wanted to send a message to another Monitor on the other side of the school, a distance of a couple of miles, he would stand on one of the many landings in these huge houses and yell,

"BOY! BOY! BOY! BOY! BOY! BOY! BOY!" The last 'Fag' to arrive would get the job.

As you got older you moved up the ladder and received new privileges that came with the office. The office of Four Yearer could be awarded to Three Yearers on merit rather than being dictated purely by the elapse of time, and with this office came the beer privilege. It would, therefore, be possible to remain a Three Yearer until you left school if your peers did not think you deserved promotion. Not only was I elected to be a Four Yearer but the House Master deemed me responsible enough to run the beer or cider allowance, which was set at four cans per week and had to be paid for out of one's stipend. This was my opportunity to get back in business after a ten-year gap.

Running the booze account involved taking orders from the boys for either beer or cider (and it *was* strictly beer or cider) and then going to the International Stores on the Harrow High street. They would process the order and deliver it to the House Master who would then ask each boy to come, collect and pay for his weekly ration. Rations not taken one week could not be carried forward to the next for obvious reasons.

Fortunately for me, International Stores went bust when one of the new big supermarkets opened in the Harrow town centre. I was given the task of finding a new supplier; a task I relished. As luck would have it, there was an off-licence at the bottom of the Hill eager for our business.

And so began the most profitable stage of my life so far. The system for ordering and delivering the booze remained the same. I had also moved into a ground floor room in the new extension of the main house miles from the House Master's quarters. My new location backed on to the rear of the London Steak House, situated next to the now defunct International Stores on Harrow-on-the-Hill High Street. The location was perfect.

It was not difficult to persuade the off-licence to open two accounts: one official and one not. Each week, their van would make two deliveries: one to the House Master as before and a much bigger one to me. I had become a sort of quasi-vintner. Anybody could order anything that the booze shop supplied: fags, gin, vodka and, on one occasion, a case of champagne. For offering this service and taking the risk, I would add on a small percentage about which everyone was totally happy.

The London Steak House proved invaluable, as not only did it offer excellent cover for the delivery van, it also did a good line in toasted sandwiches, another little earner. I was surprised that I was never caught. On Friday nights there was always a long queue outside my room. Maybe the House Master knew about it but decided to turn a blind eye? I'll never know.

Harrow was quite an extraordinary place in the early seventies; anything and everything went on. Booze, drugs, sex, fights with Hells Angels and bomb hoaxes. I never went to a school dance with the local girl schools because Harrow had been banned by every girl's school in the vicinity. My predecessors had laced the punch at one bash with vodka and three girls got pregnant. One rather mature friend of mine was expelled for screwing his twenty-five year old girlfriend in the 1st XI cricket pavilion while the following week a House Monitor was found naked with a 'Fag' in the house library in the middle of the night. He was ticked off and given a copy of *Playboy* to read. I remember hearing two stockbrokers being introduced at a cocktail party many years later.

"George… this is Simon."

"I say old chap….didn't I bugger you at school?"

We had to wear stiff collars and a boater; a ridiculous stiff straw hat that was bloody uncomfortable but made an excellent Frisbee. We also wore a black tie as we were still mourning the death of Queen Victoria! I was glad when it was all over.

Due to my business venture and frequent meetings with Miss Forbes in her mother's flat in Pimlico, my final exam results were diabolical. So my father suggested that, like him, I joined the Army.

Reluctantly I wrote to the Scots Guards and hoped that they would turn me down as I really just wanted to be a complete lazy bum. However at that time the British Army, desperately short of young officers, were interviewing everybody and anybody, so my father drove me to London for an interview at Regimental Headquarters Scots Guards, Wellington Barracks in Knightsbridge. I was cross-examined by some stuffy old Colonel who told me that if I passed the numerous and rigorous tests, then he'd be happy to welcome me to the fold. All I wanted to do was to get back to my dead-end fencing job, liar dice in the Dunne Cow public house and the large-breasted, nymphomaniac Colette, from the Belle Epoque wine bar in Knutsford. I did not win. In January 1977 I headed off to the Guards Depot in Pirbright.

After a vicious hair cut I joined the other new recruits and we were double-marched off to our barrack block to collect our kit. This was Brigade Squad: an eight week crash course in 'How to become a Guardsman'. It was designed for potential officers and was pure hell from reveille at 05:30 to whenever. We had to do the normal twenty-two week course in eight plus a bit more to prepare for the Regular Commission Board.

The RCB was a group of high-ranking officers who assessed one's ability to solve certain set tasks. This took place over three days and, if you passed, you went to the Royal Military Academy Sandhurst.

The tasks would vary. You might, for example, be given a box of matches, a banana, and a shoe lace to get you and thirty men across an alligator-infested river in twenty-five minutes – all wearing gas masks and in the middle of the night. There were a few written tests and, of course, fairly stern physical fitness tests. Apart from trying to find what is commonly referred to as 'good officer material', they were also trying to weed out the Hitler Brigade: those that love the uniform; always have the cleanest boots and equipment but could not lead a family of ducks across a fire bucket.

By now I had started to think that the Army, for a few years, might be quite fun and was secretly hoping to pass on to the next stage but I did not. Fortunately, the Army had just set up a new training division Rowallan Company. They wanted me, plus forty others to do some extra training because, although they felt we were officer material, we needed a good kick up the arse. The course lasted three months and was mainly adventure training and military style, character building exercises. On one occasion, after forty-eight hours on the move in the forests of North Wales with no food, our rations were suddenly delivered by helicopter - two live sheep! They were delicious.

After both Brigade Squad and Rowallan, Sandhurst was a walk in the park. I had opted for a three year short service commission and entered Standard Military Course 16, Salerno

Company. The Army was stuffed with protocol. Everything had to be done by the book, there were no margins, and that is why, over the next three years, I was often in trouble.

After the initial five-week breaking-in period at Sandhurst, the wife of the Commandant invited me, among others, to a cocktail party. I replied, indicating that that would be great and that I was looking forward to meeting her. A few days later, I was arrested and thrown in the Guardroom. I was marched in front of the Adjutant and very nearly thrown out of the Military altogether.

My crime? Not knowing how to reply to Lady Ward's invitation. 'Officer Cadet R. H. Miller thanks Lady Ward for her kind invitation and has much pleasure in accepting', would have been the correct form.

The rest of my time at Sandhurst was very dull apart from the final exercise on the island of Cyprus. After the exercise was over, four fellow officer cadets and I decided to get drunk. After a long lunch we hired a cheap car. We missed a hairpin bend halfway up the Troodos mountains and crashed through a barrier. A split second later the car was heading in a downward direction towards the sea but a large bush growing out of a ledge halfway down the cliff-face caught the car like a cricket ball before it went over the boundary rope for a six. Our fall was broken and the car was destroyed but, because we had all been so rubberised with booze, we survived.

Finally, on the sixth of April 1978, I passed out and joined the Second Battalion Scots Guards in Germany. My elder brother had buggered off to Argentina to work on a polo pony stud farm just outside Montevideo so I took over the Eskimo Tractor, an old Victor Volvo 121 car with about half a million miles on the clock. I packed it up with my worldly belongings and set off to war.

My new home was Wellington Barracks in Munster, North Germany. The barracks was nothing much more than a collection of old huts with the Officers mess in the middle. Apart from the guards at the gate entrance, there was nobody around. Maybe the Soviets had started something and everyone had been deployed? But that was impossible as it was a lovely Sunday afternoon and nobody goes to war on Sundays, especially if the weather is fine. I sat down in the mess and started to read a magazine when I heard footsteps coming towards the ante-room.

A man, a few years older than me with lots of short, but thick, black wavy hair, entered the room, walked up to me and shook me by the hand,

"Hi, you must be the new chap; I'm Iain Duncan-Smith."

When I saw him again years later on the telly once he had become leader of the Conservative Party, I really could not believe it was the same guy. What had happened to his hair? He must have had a terminal attack of alopecia.

We shared the barracks with a REME (Royal, Electrical and Mechanical Engineers) attachment as we were mechanised infantry soldiers. Instead of walking into battle we had APCs,(Armored Personnel Carriers), like tanks but with no gun. The idea was to drive up to the enemy, jump out of the back and then shoot them. The REME were there to fix the APCs whenever they went wrong.

The Army were in Germany to present a deterrent to the Soviets and, therefore, spent most of the time playing at being at war. Either we would go to a designated training area and kick the shit out of each other for a few weeks or we would join a huge multinational NATO force and exercise all over Germany, anywhere we liked. The former was hell as you were on the go all the time, practicing how to kill the commie bastards before they got you. The latter was far more relaxed because after each phase you had to do a damage report on what you had done to some poor German's farm. This could take ages as you would have to try and differentiate between what damage was down to you and what had been self-inflicted by the farmer, eager to boost his compensation. Once the amount of deutschmarks allocated for the manoeuvres had been used up, then it was 'END EX', time to go home. One of these huge three-week exercises lasted only six hours with a troop of American tanks destroying half a German village.

At the end of each exercise there was normally a Company Smoker. This was a massive piss-up when all ranks would adjourn to a German Gasthaus to drink copious amounts of alcohol and watch local frauleins do all sorts of things with bratwurst sausages, razor blades and ping-pong balls.

My platoon sergeant was a particularly delicate Glaswegian and on one such occasion, once finished with her bratwurst trick, the buxom beauty chopped it up and arranged the morsels on a plate which she then handed to the front row. Before any of the Guardsmen could take a piece of moist sausage the sergeant grabbed the plate.

"Where are you're fucking manners you greedy little bastards. Don't you know there's a fucking officer present?" And with that he handed me the plate. "Go on, Sir, take a few."

No sooner had I declined his kind offer, than I saw the last piece of slimy bratwurst disappear down my sergeant's gullet, much to the chagrin of the rest of my Platoon.

One year to the day after arriving in Munster it was time to leave. The whole Battalion had been posted back to Chelsea Barracks for a tour of Public Duties. This meant changing our camouflaged combat kit for red tunics, ceremonial swords and bearskins. Stationed in Chelsea we were responsible for providing the guard duties at Buckingham Palace, St James' Palace, the Tower of London and Windsor Castle.

Although a fantastic posting, Chelsea Barracks also provided plenty of opportunities for young officers to get into trouble. The only way to punish an offender was to give him extra pickets. Every day the junior officers would take it in turn to be the duty officer for the day, known as 'Picket Officer'.

This was the most thankless of tasks which involved attending all the other ranks' meals, inspecting the barracks, mounting the Guard, doing security rounds at a pre-set time during the hours of darkness and collecting any cash taken in the Sergeants' Mess that night. Full No. 2 Dress uniform had to be worn all day and mess kit in the evening. All of this had to be combined with the normal activities the Company was performing that day.

If you were late at any time or your uniform was not perfect, some bastard, who 'ated fuckin' officers' would clandestinely report you and you'd find yourself with some extra pickets the next morning at your daily debrief with the Adjutant, the scourge of all young officers. As the picket day was normally tiring it was quite easy to trip yourself up and collect a few more which inevitably had a snowball effect.

I heard one story of a young officer who turned up at some State occasion involving the Queen, the Prime Minister and the President of the USA. This officer was due to carry the Colour, however, he had left all his ceremonial kit behind and the Bandmaster had to step in. I believe the officer was given extra pickets until further notice. He did sixty-four and then went AWOL so the story goes.

I have painted a grim picture of life in Chelsea Barracks; nothing but square bashing and extra pickets. Far from it; it was a young officer's paradise. Firstly, if you were not on duty then you could get out and explore London and secondly, there were all those invitations. 'Lady Arabella Shagwell-East, for Camilla, Cocktails, 6:00pm, The Dorchester…' The Aristocracy were looking for suitable mates for their offspring and a Guards officer, if rich, was ideal.

Beside these parties, we were allowed to entertain guests while on guard at Buckingham Palace, Tower of London or Windsor Castle. The Tower and Windsor were restricted to drinks, however once the officers had finished mounting the guard at Buckingham Palace, they would adjourn to St James' Palace private rooms. Here one could entertain up to nine guests for lunch and nine for dinner. This guard consisted of three officers: the Captain of the Guard, the Subaltern, in charge of the Buckingham Palace detachment and the Ensign who carried the Colour.

The private dining room at St James' was quite magnificent with its painted ceiling, mahogany furniture and literally tons of regimental silver. Lady lunch guests were permitted but had to wear skirts or dresses of an appropriate cut and length and gentlemen guests had to wear suits. Lunch finished promptly at 3:00pm. In the evening it was men only and black tie. The menu could be anything of choice and the wines and port were normally selected by the Captain of the Guard, usually a major in rank. For young, single officers it was an excellent 'babe-magnet'.

I had fallen in lust with Peaches. Peaches was a six foot, black, American model from Los Angeles. I had met her at an art gallery in Chelsea and invited her to lunch at St James' Palace. On that particular Guard the Captain was a very charming but fastidious officer; a married man with children. Peaches arrived wearing a full-length mink coat which revealed a spray-on pink patent leather cat suit, unzipped to the naval. She greeted me with a kiss, lit a cigarette and sashayed her way up to the Captain in her leopard print stilettos.

"Hi, I'm Peaches. You must be the boss." She purred, blowing smoke rings over his head while tossing her jet black mane over one shoulder. The poor man was struck dumb. In fact we all were. None of us had ever seen anything like Peaches. In my eagerness for her to accept my invitation to lunch which would, hopefully, provide me with the all-important opportunity to lay strategic plans for our future together, I had completely forgotten to tell her the correct dress code for ladies lunching at St James' Palace.

To my astonishment the Captain of the Guard, despite his rule book mentality, did not seem to give a stuff, and at five to three he sent me a note via the orderly waiter which read; 'she can stay as long as she likes'. She very nearly became the first woman in history to dine, officially that is, at St James' Palace.

If she was in residence, you could get an invitation to dinner with The Queen and Prince Philip in Windsor Castle. An Irish Guards officer was once invited. He turned up on time, wearing: a very smart blue pinstripe suit, highly polished black brogues, and a cream shirt with a button down collar and tie. Halfway through dinner the Queen mentioned to this officer that she thought that a shirt with a stiff collar was the correct order of dress when dining at Windsor Castle.

"Oh no Ma'am, I only wear a stiff collar on important occasions."

History sadly does not relate to the number of extra pickets he received but he's probably still doing them now.

The only time I suffered with excess duties was the time of Mountbatten's murder. We had to wear black armbands when doing guard duty and I was about to march out onto the forecourt at Buckingham Palace when I noticed I hadn't got mine on. A frantic search revealed nothing so my orderly was dispatched to the Buckingham Palace kitchens and in the nick of time we stapled a rather shiny black armband, hewn from a bin liner to my tunic. It stuck out a mile and glinted in the sun and for my troubles I got seven days. However, my sentence was actually reduced from fourteen days as the bin liner episode had shown 'initiative'.

The most preposterous case of extra picketing was when a colleague of mine was given one day for not having a slice of lemon in his gin and tonic. The fact that he was allergic to citrus fruits was dismissed as bunkum and that if he could not maintain standards in the mess, he should not drink gin.

In my father's day young Guards officers could collect extras if they were seen in London without their bowler hat and carrying anything other than a black rolled up umbrella and a parcel wrapped in brown paper and white string. During inclement weather there was no question of unfurling the umbrella or dashing for cover. This was deemed to be most un-officer-like and if such rashness was replicated in a war zone, it could unsettle the other ranks. In any case, during peace time, one had one's batman or orderly to dry and press one's suits. The only permitted use for the umbrella was to hail taxis in Bond Street.

I was now two years into my three year short service commission when we received notice that a short four month, unaccompanied tour to Belfast was on the cards. South West Belfast, to be precise, the spiritual home of the IRA.

The last time I was in Northern Ireland I thought they were all mad. It was in 1968 and my parents had taken a cottage for a few weeks in the summer holidays in the quaint fishing village of Killibegs in County Donegal. The village pub was so small that the dart board was above the door. Lobsters on the quayside were ten shillings each, irrespective of the weight or size, and all the big juicy crabs were just chucked on the beach so Clunie and I would round them up before they reached the sanctuary of the sea.

G Company, 2nd Battalion Scots Guards was stationed in Glassmullen Camp, a *western* style fort but made of steel sheeting rather than wood. In a Company of approximately ninety men, there is a Company HQ, about eight men, including the company commander, normally a major in rank and the rest divided into three platoons, each headed by a junior officer, like me. One platoon guarded the camp, one went out on foot patrol in 'bricks' of four soldiers per brick and the last one remained in the camp in high speed jeeps to act as a QRF (Quick Reaction Force), ready to be called out, usually by the foot patrol, to deal with any incident.

At first I was petrified while out on foot as you are constantly thinking, *is there a sniper with me in his sights and if there is then what the hell can I do? Is that car across the road going to blow up and distribute my body parts all over the pavement?* When patrolling around high rise flats it was always important to keep an eye on the sky just in case a washing machine or car engine was dropped on your head. You had no idea who was an active member of the IRA and who was a normal member of the public because they looked the same, there was no uniform. I did not think they were quite as mad as the inhabitants of Killibegs until I was in charge of a dawn raid on a suspected terrorist's house. We had had a tip off that a badly wanted IRA member was going to be in a certain house one evening. When we smashed in the doors in the middle of the night, the stench was almost unbearable. Our terrorist was asleep on the kitchen floor along with about ten others. The living room was the same, in total about twenty people. Nobody slept upstairs. Halfway up the stairs we realised why. The steady flow of excrement from the toilet, sink and finally the bath was slowly taking over the house.

Apart from the murder of my Commanding Officer of my Brigade Squad, Richard Westmacott, who had joined the SAS, our tour was reasonably uneventful. The only soldier we lost was on the Troop ship on the way back to Liverpool. A Guardsman got so drunk he fell overboard and despite going round in circles for hours we never found him.

There were, however, two highly amusing incidents that really made me chuckle. The first one involved a Guardsman. While out on patrol one night he found himself with his trousers round his ankles, pressed up against a tennis court type fence with his dick sticking through. On the other side a young Irish girl had dropped her knickers, lifted her skirt and backed onto his dick. Through the fence he was holding one end of a five pound note and she the other. He was caught by one of my fellow officers and when told to stop what he was doing immediately he bellowed in a broad Glaswegian accent, "Och Sir, let me cum me duff first!"

The officer agreed, the shot was fired and the girl disappeared into the darkness, five pounds better off.

The second incident could only have been orchestrated by a government department, in this case, the Ministry of Defence. Some fat 'overlunched' minister, had decided that troops in Northern Ireland were unable to keep up their fitness levels due to the nature of the job so the camps were to be given squash courts at a cost of £150,000 each. Glassmullen Camp was going to be the pilot scheme and in no time at all we had a squash court. We could not use it because the builders had left a cement mixer inside the court and the door was too narrow to wheel it out. Instead of taking the machine to pieces, which might have taken an hour or two at the most, the MOD had the roof taken off and the mixer winched out by crane. The roof was replaced and we started to play squash. A day later we heard that the forces in Belfast were going to be reduced and some camps demolished. The first camp to go was Glassmullen and by the end of that week the wreckers arrived and demolished both the camp and the squash court.

Our tour over, we returned to Public Duties at Chelsea Barracks and the Charles and Diana Royal Wedding. Everyone was eager to be involved in the parades, Guards and street-lining. All except me. Army life was becoming tiresome. The main problem was there was no risk/reward ratio. It did not matter what you did or how well or badly you did it, your pay was the same.

I was eager to see if I could make it as a salesman in the real world. After the Royal Wedding I was about to hand in my notice when a four month tour of Kenya was announced. The Kenyan Government liked to have a British Army presence to deter potential aggressors such as the Sudanese. We flew to Nairobi, via Cyprus from RAF Brize Norton and, as the most senior officer on board my plane, I was made 'IC Plane' (in charge of). Halfway to Cyprus an army Captain approached me and announced in a very pompous manner that the General wanted to talk to me immediately. He was sitting in the RAF's version of first class and demanded to see my wet weather programme, my contingency plans.

"What plans had you in mind sir?" I inquired.

"Crash plans," he yelled, "What are you going to do if the plane crashes?"

"Die, Sir?" I offered. He did not think that it was very funny and found it less amusing when I pointed out that if the G force did not rip our heads off, then the mountain we were bound to hit, probably would.

We arrived in Nairobi and then drove to the base camp at Nanuki which had already been set up by the Advance Party. Whenever the Army travels there is always an Advance Party and a Rear Party. The Advance Party sets up camp and the Rear Party dismantles it. The Rear Party mostly comprises of soldiers who need time to recover from social ailments contracted from the local whores before going home to their wives.

My first task in Kenya was to take my platoon down to the Masai Mara and set up camp next to a Safari Lodge. We were to help the Kenyan Government build sixty concrete triangulation stations across the Mara, so the tribes would finally know what land was theirs and what land belonged to the Safari Lodges. The Kenyan architect was due to arrive the following morning with all the details of where they should be built. The building materials had already arrived. By noon the next day he had still not arrived and I was beginning to worry. Maybe he'd been scoffed by a lion? Finally, at 5:00pm, he turned up as pissed as a rat.

"Terribly sorry I'm so late," he slurred, "but my jeep broke down. Let's go to the Lodge bar and discuss what's going on huh?"

This happened every day for a week and, in our allotted time, we only built one station. Just before we left the Mara he invited me to join him at the bar.

"I hope I'm not going to get you into trouble for the apparent lack of activity, but let me ask you this question. If you were paid by the hour and not sure of any future work once a project was completed wouldn't you drag it out for as long as possible?"

After a few weeks of pretending to kill Russians I went down to the coast near Mombasa and stayed at the Ocean Sports Club, locally referred to as the Open Shorts Club. It was run by an English couple and a delicious French waitress who reminded me of the lovely Colette I had abandoned in Knutsford.

Above the bar there were fish trophies; heads of marlins and sharks all caught off the local boat, Honeylulu. I hired the boat with an American and two Australians and we set off into the Indian Ocean in search of big fish. Nothing happened all day, apart from catching the odd kingfish and a few rainbow runners, so we headed back to the shore. One of the Australians decided to have a last go and within seconds he'd hooked something big. The line flew out and moments later a marlin leapt out of the water. The Aussie strapped himself into the fishing chair and fought the fish for about half an hour before it gave up and he started to reel it in. We were just about to enter the bay when suddenly the marlin seemed to come alive. The line shot out again, but this time much harder and faster. Three hours later and utterly exhausted we strapped an 803lb tiger shark to the back of the boat.

My delightful week's holiday was over and the only way back to Mombasa was by mini bus. This was no ordinary bus as it stopped *everywhere* and the passenger list included sheep, dogs, goats and chickens. Despite these unscheduled detours, no one ever got off, just more people and their menagerie tried to get in or on. People climbed on the roof, and each time the bus went round a corner, a few fell off, bouncing down the road and ending in a ditch, apparently none the worse for wear. I was lucky, apart from the chicken that sat on my lap from Open Shorts to Mombasa, I had a seat.

Advised to travel first class on the train back to Nanuki, I had previously made a reservation. My cabin was like a room in a five star hotel. Linen sheets, fresh fluffy towels and, no sooner had I unpacked than there was a knock on the door and a train steward entered wearing a starched blue uniform with highly polished brass buttons, carrying a silver tray. I ordered a gin and tonic (with lemon just in case) and a few minutes later it arrived in a beautiful cut glass crystal tumbler.

Twenty minutes later he returned to announce that my table was ready in the dining car. The dining car was equally impressive; wooden panelling, linen table cloths, silver candle sticks on each table and silver cutlery. The fillet steak was delicious and I retired to bed with a large whisky and soda. After bacon and eggs for breakfast I was met at the station and driven back to Nanuki.

When the final exercise was over, two other officers and I were offered the chance to drive around Kenya for two weeks by my Commanding Officer. As far as the MOD were concerned we were on a PR exercise to make sure our soldiers had not left any problems behind. In reality it was an all-expenses paid holiday. We met up with the White Mischief Brigade, Sam Weller and Digby Tatum-Walters, to name a few and went on some spectacular safaris.

A lonely botanist, who lived on the edge of Lake Baringo with his wife and two small children, had heard about our trip and sent us a telegram begging us to visit. He welcomed us with open arms and barbequed the '*fatted*' catfish which we washed down with Tusker beer on their veranda, only about twenty feet from the water's edge.

After the meal, while we were drinking coffee and sipping cognac, a very large hippo emerged from the lake and started munching grass. Our host reassured us that as long as we did not get in between the hippo and the water it did not present any danger.

The beast carried on grazing and slowly moved round the side of the bungalow. We continued chatting and drinking and quite forgot about it. Suddenly we heard a scream from the children's room so we all rushed in and found them standing on their beds like starfish, covered in what only can be described as runny spinach. In fact the whole room was covered in runny spinach. The hippopotamus, while still eating, had backed up to their bedroom window and farted.

The next morning, after 'Operation Spinach Cleanup' had been completed, we returned to the Aberdare Country Club where Sam Weller had arranged for us to go on a night buffalo shoot. This was at the request of a local farmer as a herd was destroying his fences and crops. One night, armed with a rifle which used a bullet the size of a Havana cigar, we set off in search of this herd in an open-top Land Rover with searchlights. After about half an hour we found the herd, drove into the middle of it and shot the biggest bugger we could see. The recoil nearly ripped my friend's arm off but his aim was good and the black monster dropped like a stone. All the Africans jumped out and started hacking the buffalo's head off and, once severed, they put it in the Land Rover and we drove off, leaving the rest of it as a reminder.

We spent the last two days of our freebie at the Muthega Club in Nairobi. A very old colonial establishment full of old men sitting in wicker chairs, reading *The Times*, farting and drinking pink gin. The accommodation wasn't up to much but I had the best roast beef and Yorkshire pudding I had, up until then, ever eaten.

The final job I had to do before I left the Army was run a small exercise near Catterick in Northumberland. The day we got there it started to snow very heavily and by the second day we were snowed in along with the entire little village next to the barracks. The exercise was cancelled but we found a projector and some old films in the gymnasium, so we set up a small makeshift cinema and invited the villagers and the primary school. The film rolled and, to my horror, the first scene was a girl pleasuring a man in the toilet of a train. By the time the projectionist had found the off switch, '*Debbie does Catterick*' had made its mark. For me, however, it was too late for extra pickets as my time in Her Majesty's Forces was up.

Chapter Two

Before leaving the Army I did have the opportunity to sign on for another year in order to get shot at by Argies in the Falkland Islands, but it didn't have quite the same appeal as a trip to Kenya so I declined the kind offer. My plan was to get a job as a salesman and make loads of money.

My first idea was to become an account executive with a leading advertising agency in London. I did not get a single reply. Next I tried estate agents. One interview with a large red-faced pig dressed in a pinstripe suit but no job.

My army gratuity was running low when, out of the blue, I received a letter from my old pal, Sam. He had gone out to Australia and suggested I joined him so I did. We moved into a two bedroom flat in Double Bay, Sydney and I started looking for work. Rather than write letters I thought I would just walk into an office and demand employment. This did not take long. Bondi Junction was only a five minute walk up the hill from our flat and at the top, the first office I came to was an estate agency called Laing & Simmonds. This was run by a short, fat Aussie called Peter and he, no doubt out of idle curiosity, offered me a job on the spot.

The office was divided into two departments; house sales and strata management. Apart from me and the sales manager, Peter only employed gorgeous girls which obviously irritated his wife. The prettiest and sexiest was Shauna. She had everything, including a very jealous husband who dropped her off in the morning, met her for lunch and picked her up at the end of the working day.

Later that year, after the Christmas party date was confirmed, I asked Peter what normally happened at the Laing & Simmonds parties?

"Well mate, we usually hire a bloody big motor boat, cruise down to Rose Bay, drink a lot of tinnies, get shit-faced and all try and fuck Shauna."

Peter put me on the strata management side of the business. In Sydney there were lots of condominiums and the owners would form a committee and appoint a managing agent, me. It was not a sales job, as such, but it taught me how to deal with people as I would frequently have to come between feuding committee members who rarely agreed on anything. The subjects would vary from whether they should re-paint the whole block at vast expense down to 'can Kylie have a cat flap?' It was always the smallest issues that caused the biggest problems.

As jobs went, it was shit but paid me just enough to allow me to indulge in what most red-blooded twenty-three-year-old boys like doing; drinking beer, eating steak, chasing girls and visiting booth number nine in the Love Art shop with Miss Coutts.

When my working holiday visa expired the Aussies would not renew it so I had to return to the United Kingdom. This was probably a good thing as it was time to get back into the real world and start looking for a serious career. I landed in London, rented a room in Fulham and got a part-time job delivering fancy shirts to toffs in the City. The firm, based in Lotts Road, was Workshop Clothing Ltd. and they employed a team of Sloane Ranger girls, going around offices, selling Jermyn Street style shirts (Turnbull & Asser, New & Lingwood, etc.), at TK Maxx prices.

My role was to deliver the shirts and collect the money; not always easy. One very fat and pompous stockbroker had ordered over £400 worth of shirts but I would not accept his cheque as he had no cheque guarantee card.

"Listen here, you young puppy," he bellowed, "I'm a stockbroker and my word is my bond."

"Look you great tub of lard, no card, no shirts, geddit?" I replied. Not true. I actually asked him if I could telephone my office to authorise me to accept his cheque without a card. Because his name was Sebastian Ponsonby-Fortescue-Sweatalot, they agreed. Needless to say the cheque was of the rubber variety and Workshop Clothing Ltd. bounced into administration shortly afterwards too, so I was told.

Delivering shirts to overpaid and rude fat bastards in the City was not my idea of a career so I was constantly scanning the appointment sections. One day, while thumbing through the *Daily Telegraph*, I saw one that jumped out of the page and smacked me right across my face.

'Wanted, 22-25-year-olds to train as Financial Advisors for a major independent firm, would suit ex-army officers.'

Wow! My perfect job. £50,000 a year here we come. I rang the number and got an interview immediately. The next day I took the train to Windsor and after a brief chat was offered a place on the next training course which was due to start in September. A basic salary of £9,000 per annum plus commission and a Ford Escort 1.3 company car. I had arrived!

The training course took place at the Holiday Inn, Heathrow Airport, and lasted three weeks. There were twenty of us on day one and by day two our number had dwindled to fifteen. We were the new tin of sardines and I quickly struck up a friendship with two of my fellow fish, Nick and Anton. Nick was ex-army and ex-RAF. Anton was the local Windsor wide boy.

During the course we had been taught all about investments, tax, insurance and general financial planning and now, after only three weeks, we were going to be let loose on the poor and unsuspecting, highly vulnerable, general public. We were the new batch of highly trained Independent Financial Advisors, each with a business card and a shitty car to prove it.

We got our leads from equivocal advertisements that the firm placed in the national press. These adverts were designed to lure punters by offering fanciful returns on certain types of investments. Our job was to follow up the enquiries and make appointments to go and see these prospects and then flog them whatever was flavour of the month. Talking of flavour, we always sold the products issued by the insurance companies who took us out for the longest lunches.

Nick, Anton and I, when we were not driving all over the country, divesting little old ladies of their life savings, could be found in the 'Chimp and Vibrator', normally known as the Two Brewers in Windsor. They served good food and an excellent drop of Directors Bitter. In the 80s everybody drank at lunch times and nobody batted an eyelid at driving a car after quaffing gallons of ale. Sometimes our lunches would go on for hours, so Anton and I decided to buy a house in Windsor which we could all use for our post-lunch *sports afternoons*.

Anton had a very neurotic girlfriend who was causing him a great deal of unnecessary grief so he decided to bugger off to Portugal and try his hand in the timeshare business. Six months later I went out to see him. He was raking it in and suggested that I should stay and join him, but my parochial upbringing got the better of me so I returned to Windsor. Maybe a big mistake?

Nick and I continued to underachieve in Windsor and by now my elder brother, Clunie had found himself a Portuguese wife, had some kids and was running an import/export textile business in Portugal. My younger brother, Julian was coping as best as he could.

Julian, or Jules as he was known, was born with a rare blood disease called Haemophilia. A Haemophiliac's blood lacks Factor VIII (FVIII), the essential blood-clotting protein which makes sufferers easily prone to internal bleeding, bruising as it is more commonly referred to. Unlike normal people, the internal bleeding with a haemophiliac can take much longer to stop so the joints near the source fill up with blood, causing abnormal swelling and excruciating pain. For example, if my brother cut himself, the bleed could go on for days, even weeks without stopping. Mini-haemorrhages could also happen at random and without warning. There was and still is no cure for Haemophilia.

When Julian was small, each time a bleed started, my parents would take him to Pendlebury Children's Hospital in Manchester, where he would be fed by an intravenous drip synthetic FVIII and, depending upon the severity of the bleed, could spend up to two weeks in hospital. This was a very expensive non-permanent treatment and relied wholly on the blood-donating fraternity in the United Kingdom. However, as there was not enough blood, more had to be imported, mainly from America, where people were paid to donate. This reward system attracted society's 'desperados', in particular, the drug addicts.

Jules spent much of his childhood dipping in and out of hospital and his legs were frequently immobilised in plaster casts as his knees were especially vulnerable. Ramps were installed at home to cater for his wheelchair and as swimming was very good for him, all emphasis was placed on summer holidays. Skiing was out of the question. He was frequently in great pain and would often wake in the night, screaming. On those occasions all we could do was to apply ice packs and witch-hazel to numb the discomfort as much as possible.

After one particularly bad episode when he was about seven years old, my parents took him to the South of France for a special treat. One day he was hobbling down the beach when he was stopped by a middle-aged American lady who was sunbathing with her husband within earshot of my parents.

"What's your name little boy?" she asked.

"Julian," he replied.

"Tell me, why are you limping? Did you hurt yourself playing football?"

"No," said Julian, "I'm a haemophiliac."

"Well, gee, I think that's absolutely marvellous."

As he grew, the frequency of his bleeds increased, but despite this my parents were hell-bent on ensuring he led as normal a life as possible, so he joined me at the Dragon School in Oxford. By sheer chance the Haemophilia Centre was based at the Nuffield Orthopedic Centre which was on the outskirts of Oxford. Frequent visits here interrupted his studies but, with fantastic support from the school, he did very well academically, narrowly missing a Scholarship to Harrow, gaining an Exhibition instead.

Sadly, Harrow were unable to replicate the Dragon success, so when I left so did he. He was now fourteen and tutored at home. Physically this was very good for him, but socially it was a disaster and he went to the local school in Winsford, Cheshire to do his 'O' and 'A' levels.

Suddenly there was a medical breakthrough for haemophiliacs. 'Home' treatment had arrived and virtually consigned hospital visits to the bin. Julian now received his FVIII plasma in dried form in little bottles. Along with these bottles came distilled water and needles. Whenever he felt the need he would give himself a 'fix', just like a junkie.

He was now eighteen and fully grown. The bruising problem in his joints had reduced slightly but over the years his knees had been so badly damaged, arthritis came to the party.

Jules' 'A' Level results were good enough to secure a place at Birmingham University, equidistant between his Oxford clinic and our parents' new home in North Wales. Jules shared a flat above a farmhouse with his new friend, John Seagrim. John made Julian's life at Birmingham University possible, and whenever I could, I would go and stay with them after dishing out some *best advice* to some little old lady in the area. Instead of spending my expenses on hotels I used to buy wholly inappropriate food and wine for large pig-outs with Jules and John.

Jules cut quite a dash and was beginning to attract a few female admirers but he deliberately put them off because, although he had the same urges as most young heterosexual men, he felt that his body would let him down. He once told me, after a rather drunken dinner, that he didn't dare have a wank in case it started a haemorrhage; therefore a shag was out of the question.

John's presence had given Julian a false sense of security and a confidence that could only be sustained when they lived together. John did everything for him; for Jules it was like having a private butler.

When they both finished at university, John went to work in London and Jules got a job with the advertising agency, McCann Ericsson in Solihull. He was determined that he was going to be independent and to this end he moved into a cottage on the Packington Estate near Coventry. At the beginning everything was fine, but soon he found it too hard and his body started to fail him. The more he tried to work, the sicker he became and started missing deadlines. McCann Ericsson bent over backwards to help him, but they had to run a profitable business, so by mutual consent he left.

Realistically, Julian only had one option: To return to the sanctuary of my parents home in Wales to lick his wounds and fathom out what to do next. My father had always been a keen shot. He had shot grouse in Derbyshire, pheasants and duck in Wales, stags in Scotland and wild boar in Austria. He was getting on a bit and decided to give up shooting, but when he heard that London Zoo were getting rid of their wild boar because they were no longer considered a viable 'zoo attraction', he rang them up to see if he could buy them. 'Big

Dave', as he became known, was going to become the first breeder of pure wild boar in this country.

'Mr Miller, if you can come and collect them and assure us that you have accommodation for them that complies with the Dangerous Wild Animals Act 1978, then you can have them for nothing', was their response. Most probably, the alternative fate for these beasts was the Croydon cat food factory. Big Dave quickly converted a few barns and the boars arrived from London zoo. Anton bought my stake of the Windsor house as I decided to move to Wales to help with the wild boar, the new family business.

It was 1986 and Jules was only twenty-three years old. Although he was financially secure as he had the full entitlement to disability benefits and since he was living at home, it suddenly dawned on him that he was totally reliant on others to make his life bearable. My parents looked after him completely. He did try and spend some time in Portugal with Clunie, but he and his wife had a young family and a fledgling business, so Jules returned to Wales.

Naturally he became quite depressed. All his peers had jobs, were in relationships and were living normal lives, but he was restricted to his prison in North Wales. Although he had regular visits from John and others he felt that he was living a non-life, a life without direction or purpose. His physical problems were reasonably stable due to his lack of activity, but he still had to inject himself once or twice a week to keep it that way. Prophylactic treatment did not guarantee a bleed-free life.

While Jules was doing the *Daily Telegraph* crossword every day I was busy trying to make the wild boar shag each other. I bought them copies of *Playboar* to get them in the mood and it finally worked. Soon we had lots of stripy boarlets running all over the place. To supplement the boar business, I built a smokehouse. Here I smoked fish and chicken which I sold to local restaurants and pubs.

But things were about to change for my little brother. In 1972 Britain started to import unscreened Factor VIII from America for the first time. However, in 1974 the Health Secretary declared that, if enough money was invested, then the United Kingdom would soon be self-sufficient in blood products. This did not happen, and successive governments continued to import 'dirty blood.'

The haemophiliacs needed a regular supply of fresh blood. It was not an option *not* to take the blood medication and with this treatment HIV and AIDS had now arrived; a catastrophe for the haemophiliacs. A few weeks later Julian learned that he had the dreaded HIV virus. And in a cruel twist, Jules had also just found a wonderful girl who actually went to her GP and said that she was considering sleeping with a HIV positive haemophiliac, not someone with the full blown disease, just the virus. The GP would have been struck off if he had advised this and, quite naturally, the relationship foundered. One by one haemophiliacs were being diagnosed with the AIDS virus and in no time at all, numbered twelve hundred. Every day several of these would develop the full-blown disease which meant certain death; maybe not immediately, but it was inevitable. Some died quite quickly and some lingered on.

Haemophiliacs were losing their jobs; they couldn't get mortgages or life insurance and the ignorance of the general public led them to believe that anyone with AIDS must be a drug addict, a prostitute or gay. As a result of this rank stupidity, a few haemophiliacs were driven out of their own communities and branded as lepers. Others were beaten up, verbally abused in public and had dog shit pushed through their letter boxes. It rapidly became a very serious problem and got worse each day as more and more sufferers were being diagnosed with the virus. Something had to be done and done very quickly.

Considering it took more than twenty years for the Government to admit responsibility for the Thalidomide fiasco and start paying compensation, it only took the Haemophilia Society three weeks to get its first big payment. Jules headed the campaign to seek compensation and, after a private meeting with John Moore, the Secretary of State for Health in Thatcher's Government, an immediate payment of ten million pounds was made and the MacFarlane Trust was up and running. This was classified as an '***ex-gratia***' payment and ***not*** compensation. "Okay, we'll give you haemophiliacs a little bit of money, (to make us look good and hope you will all just go away) but it's not our fault... so there!"

However, this was not nearly enough, even for the twelve hundred haemophiliacs already infected. What about the rest and those yet to be born? There was no way the Government was going to get away with this 'quick fix' approach long-term. It was disgusting.

Jules continued his campaign and appeared on the television, in the newspapers and on the radio. He was perfect for the job as he had had some media training while working at McCann Ericsson. One day he got a phone call from Noreen Bray, who presented, *Week in Week Out*, for BBC Wales. She had seen Jules chatting with Dr. Hilary Jones on 'Good Health' and decided that, to help the campaign, she would make a documentary about him, his illness and the struggle to get more money from the government. Noreen and her crew came up to North Wales and it took them four days to complete. It was a great success as it helped reboot the campaign. We had hundreds of letters, and Jules made more TV appearances. The *Sunday Times* decided to really beat up the government who then coughed up another £20,000 each for the infected haemophiliacs and then closed the till.

At this time, the wild boar breeding and the smoking business was not working as the whole episode with the Jules campaign meant that I had taken my eye off the ball, so I decided to get back into the financial services industry. My father sold the remaining boar and Jules stayed in Wales and continued working with the Haemophilia Society which now had the problem of how to distribute all the money. He was still sitting on the time bomb and every time he got a slight cold or an upset stomach he would think that maybe '*this was it*'.

One day, to relieve his boredom, I took him to one of my friend's wedding and, as his knees were not good that day, we took the wheelchair. At the wedding reception a woman, who we had never met before, came up to him, put her nose right in his face and shouted very slowly:

"CAN I GET YOU AN ORANGE DRINK?"

"No, you condescending bitch," he barked. "Fuck off and get me some champagne."

I have never understood why people assume that if someone is in a wheelchair they must be deaf, mentally challenged and tee-total. It was not a very good wedding, as I recall, so we left shortly afterwards.

Via a headhunter in Manchester I was offered an ideal job back in the financial services sector and I was able to get home often to be with my good mate, Jules. The job in Manchester was not so, 'off the hoof' as the one in Windsor as the industry was now being looked at very carefully. Far too many complaints were being made. The regulators were sharpening their teeth so we all had to be very compliant and really give good advice, not just the advice that paid the most commission. The company I joined was small. Head office in London was run by the most unpleasant man I have ever met and the Manchester office run by an affable twit.

Meanwhile, back on the farm, Jules was just pottering about with the Haemophilia Society and entertaining friends at weekends. He had also started to write about his experiences, but he found this quite difficult as the constant one finger bashing on the word processor would start bleeds in his right hand so he would have to stop. He tried using his other fingers and his left hand but with the same result, so in the end he gave up.

Although I had now bought a flat in Manchester I still went back to Wales once a week and virtually every weekend. One Sunday in late September 1990, Jules got up in the middle of lunch and retired to bed feeling a bit off-colour. We were quite used to this behaviour and thought no more about it.

Chapter Three

The following day I had a meeting in Stafford. I had just passed Knutsford Service Station when my car telephone rang. It was my brother calling from Portugal.

"Rupes, hi it's Clunie. Jules woke this morning with a hell of a fever. He's got double pneumonia and they think it's full blown AIDS. He has been taken to Liverpool Royal Hospital by ambulance."

"SHIT!"

"Mother's at the hospital and we need to get hold of Daddy. I believe he's at a meeting near Preston."

"Okay, I will track him down and call you later. Love to Sylvia and the kids, bye."

I got off the motorway at the next junction and pulled into the first parking place. I rang the office and asked them to cancel my meetings and told them I would be off for a few days.

My father was at a charity meeting at a hotel just outside Preston and fortunately I knew the number of a solicitor who was at the same meeting. A few minutes later his secretary gave me the number for the hotel.

"Hello, can I speak to a Mr. David Miller please; he's lunching with you today with the Booth Charity Trust." My father knew immediately what was wrong.

"It's Jules, he's got double pneumonia and they think it is the real thing. Mother is at the Royal Liverpool Hospital.

I suggest you go there and take her home. I am coming over there now and will call you from the hospital. Okay?"

"Okay." he spluttered. I later found out that my father had collapsed on hearing the news. I drove to Liverpool and got to the Royal Liverpool Hospital early afternoon. Jules was in Ward 7Y. Thank god he had a room of his own. He was not conscious, barely breathing and had tubes coming out of everywhere. He was extremely ill.

I sat with him for about five hours. Every now and again he'd open one eye and smile. At about 8:00pm I left and on my way out I asked Debbie, the duty nurse, what was going to happen. She didn't really know but said, in a roundabout way, that his chances of surviving the night were about 50/50. That night I stayed with some old friends, Nick and Sarah Stanley, who lived in a lovely Georgian house in Falkner Street not far from the hospital.

Nick woke me with a cup of tea and after breakfast I went straight round to the hospital fearing the worst, but he'd survived the night and was sitting up in bed quite awake. My parents were in absolute pieces, particularly my father. He did not have any idea on how to deal with this. My mother was much stronger on the outside but the anguish in her eyes betrayed her. For some reason I was quite calm but we all knew that this was the beginning of the end. Jules had joined the queue.

My brother had two doctors assigned to him. Charles Hay and 'Gorg'O' Doc'. Charlie Hay was a leading AIDS specialist and 'Gorg'O' Doc' was his very pretty assistant. She was a gorgeous doctor and we gave her this eponymous title after the Spud 'U' Like theme. It was very puerile but it amused us.

With the guidance of these two quacks Jules now embarked on a massive anti-AIDS drug campaign and in no time at all he recovered from the pneumonia. The next problem he had to deal with was the side-effects of the drugs.

He developed rashes, bed sores and lost his appetite. His temperature fluctuated wildly and he was constantly being sick. My parents prepared him delicious snacks and we used to have picnics in his room but he ate little. They found it very difficult going to see him, and could only bear short visits. The situation was clearly tearing them apart. You're supposed to die before your offspring not after.

Jules mainly wanted company and John Seagrim visited a great deal. Another friend called Sarah Reid used to hop on the train from London to Liverpool on a regular basis too. I used to go and see him as much as I could and, according to my boss, far too much. One of us would sit with him for hours not saying anything, just being there for him in case he wanted to talk. Sometimes he was quite chatty and other times he was just sad.

Whether it was the drugs or his visits or whatever, Jules began to get better and, much to my parents' delight, his appetite returned a little. Although he was literally half the man he used to be, Charlie Hay decided that it was time for him to go home. His physical appearance changed in other ways too. I don't know why but, for some reason, during his stay in hospital his eyelashes had grown very long and his blue eyes had become icy and clear.

It was a huge relief for him to get back home and he spent most of his days in bed with Musket, his incredibly spoilt cavalier King Charles spaniel. My parents continued to toil in the kitchen to produce something that he would actually eat but rarely succeeded.

I had spent a great deal of time at the Royal Liverpool Hospital and had neglected my job so I wasn't too surprised when my boss fired a warning shot across my bows. As Jules was now back at home I thought I better fall back into line and get on with some work. I found this very difficult, and when I was invited to stay with some old friends in Suffolk I jumped at it.

The weekend revolved around the Aldeburgh Yacht Club Dance and my blind date was Sally, a divorcee with two small children. Two months later, on the twelfth of December 1990, we got married in London and Jules came down to be my best man.

Shortly afterwards I parted company with the Manchester crew and found employment with another independent financial advisor in London, close to my new marital home. My new wife, inherited children and I spent Christmas that year with my parents and Jules in North Wales. Christmas was fairly subdued and we did not celebrate New Year. In fact, come to think of it, I think we were all in bed by 10:30pm.

The Sunday night before we were due to head back to London Jules developed a very high temperature, so we bundled him into my car and I sped him back to Ward 7Y.

While they were able to deal with the pneumonia what they could not do was predict what was going to develop next. The problem with AIDS is that it has the ability to mutate, slowly but surely destroying the immune system until nothing is left.

Over the next six to eight months Jules went in and out of hospital on a regular basis. He grew weaker and weaker and got thinner and thinner. By now the local GP, Tecwyn Jones had become involved and both he and Charlie Hay agreed that Jules should really remain at home so he could die with dignity.

He was slowly beginning to develop a form of Alzheimer's disease and started talking gibberish. John continued to visit; as did Sarah Reid and he had both a day and night nurse. We would sit with him, and every now and again, he'd suddenly sit up in bed, tell us all to 'fuck off' and then fall back onto his side. He existed, nothing more, and his weight had dropped to five stone from fourteen. He was grey in colour and his eyelashes seemed to be getting even longer. He was no longer the man I knew and loved. He was an empty shell.

Jules had a morphine cassette attached to the right side of his body. This was a cute little machine that injected morphine at pre-determined times to reduce the suffering. We were now in the home stretch. I thought, not long to go now Jules, you'll soon be free.

For three days Jules had no fluids or solids and Tecwyn was amazed that he was still alive. We were expecting him to go at any time. Another weekend passed and still he held on. Monday, Tuesday, Wednesday and Thursday all came and went but Jules was still alive.

On Friday night we were all sitting downstairs watching television. Tecwyn was upstairs with Jules. It was about 8:15pm and I suddenly got up and decided to go and see my brother. I do not know why, I just did. It was dark in his room and he was barely breathing. He certainly did not know I was in the room. Tecwyn was sitting on the other side of the bed.

Jules suddenly opened one eye, tried to smile and then closed it. At that moment the last remaining sheen left his skin and he died. Tecwyn quickly confirmed that he was dead and asked me if I'd like him to tell everyone downstairs.

"No thanks Tecwyn, I'll do it."

We walked down the stairs together and into the sitting room. I stood in the entrance and just said, "It's over, he's gone." It was a Friday, the sixth of December 1991.

I cannot really remember what happened next except that the undertakers arrived to take Jules away and when they did I felt very relieved and very calm. It wasn't until months later that the shock of my brother's death really hit me.

The funeral was held in the local village and the wake took place in the most wonderful Country House Hotel and Restaurant, Tyddyn Llan, run by good friends, Peter and Bridgit Kindred. We weren't sure how many people were going to turn up for the funeral so we asked Peter and Bridgit to make lashings of both cottage and fish pie and lay on plenty of house wine.

Well over 200 people turned up to see Julian off, some we had not seen for twenty years or more and virtually everyone was in floods of tears. The service was beautifully conducted by 'Two Helpings' Canon Jones and Prebendary Alan Tanner. Canon Jones was the local Welsh Official and Alan Tanner was present as his son was also a haemophiliac facing the same fate as Jules.

Julian arrived in a small coffin; he didn't need a big one and it was carried by the postmaster, his son, an undertaker and our next door farmer. After the service we buried him in the village cemetery and then walked down the country lane to the hotel. Just as we were all strolling down the road a farmer decided to move his flock of sheep down the same road but in the opposite direction. In no time at all mourners and ewes mingled and the poor farmer was very distraught that he had upset a funeral. However, we did assure him that as we were unable to get an RAF fly-past from the boys at RAF Valley in Anglesey, a sheep-past was the next best thing.

Canon Jones was a very large Welshman with a huge appetite. Not only did he help himself to two helpings of cottage pie, he also had two helpings of fish pie and those are only the ones we noticed. In addition, his thirst was on the same level but seemed totally sober when he left. The party at the hotel went on for hours as nobody wanted to leave. We were all chatting about Jules and thinking about how best to remember him.

Sir George Christie, the owner of the opera house, Glyndebourne, suggested that we erect a large sundial in the Glyndebourne Gardens as Jules was a great opera fan and had spent part of his time, while he was ill, as a guest of the Christie family at Glyndebourne. The cost of this dial was estimated at over £6,000 so John Seagrim volunteered to be in charge of fundraising. In no time at all donations came in and the dial was built.

So my best friend was dead and I was back in London with my wife, two step-daughters and a pet rabbit. My new sales position was based in Bond Street and the independent financial advisor I worked for concentrated on providing income for the recently retired.

The only reason I got the job was that I had put 'wild boar breeder' on my Curriculum Vitae. It stood out a mile among all the other applications the company had received and so they decided, despite the crap references from my previous employer, to give me a chance.

This was my first commission only position. No sale no pay. To date it was the best job I'd ever had. The company advertised furiously all over the UK and had built up a network of offices ranging from Inverness to Plymouth. The enquiries came into head office by the bucketload and they were dealt out according to your area of operations. Mine was Central and North London. I would visit customers in their homes and offices to try and persuade them to invest their tax-free lump sum from their pension fund, plus any other savings they might have accumulated over the years, into one of our income and growth plans in order to supplement their company pensions.

I became good at this quite quickly as being a self-employed commission only salesman got me out of bed far quicker than before and my bank account duly blossomed.

After about six months two things happened: My brother's death hit me in the back of the head like a sledgehammer and I suddenly realised that I did not nor had I ever loved my wife. When I went to that party in Suffolk I was an emotional wreck looking for any port in a storm and she seemed to be that haven. On reflection I think she might have been looking for the same.

Depression and alcohol began to visit me in equal measures and, as a result my work suffered and we started to fight. To avoid these fights I used to come home very late and go straight to bed. She accused me of having affairs and seeing prostitutes, but having seen my brother die of a disease that was often associated with sex, that line of attack was way off the mark. One day she rang me in the office and told me that if I was not going to get my act together then I might as well leave. So I did.

After I hung up the most enormous sense of relief engulfed my entire being. I had just made an excellent decision. I had very little money and nowhere to stay but I felt terrific. I didn't want to call any of my tried and trusted friends as they would have told me to be sensible, call my wife, apologise for being a selfish dickhead and go home. Instead I went into hiding and stayed with numerous people all over London.

During this house hopping my attendance at work deteriorated as did my mental health. I had a horrific recurring nightmares where Jules kept escaping from his coffin, and after recovering his full health he was killed in a car crash. The only way to block these dreams was to increase my alcohol intake but this led to mind-numbing hangovers and the inability to work. It was no surprise when I was invited by the company for an interview *without* coffee.

A few months later I was mildly amused to read that they had too been forced out of business for irregular practices. Nothing like a bit of gratuitous schadenfreude to boost one's spirits. Before the company ceased trading they mistakenly paid me £4,000 in commission on a cancelled deal so I retreated to North Wales with a smile like a Cheshire cat. I stopped boozing and started to sleep like a baby, but my mind was still in turmoil. I couldn't come to terms with my brother's death so I used to visit his grave and get really angry with him for letting me down so badly. It was so bloody selfish and downright inconvenient for him to die like that. What in the fuck was I supposed to do now, huh?

It became a dangerous ritual and many times I felt like joining him. Why not? Maybe it was better on the other side? Who knew? I also started to blame myself, not for his death, but for his suffering. If I had not sat with him and held his hand the first night he was admitted to the Royal Liverpool, then maybe he would have slipped away then? All the 'what ifs' raced round my mind chasing their own tails until they became so dizzy I thought I would explode.

Most men avoid the doctor just in case the news is bad. However, something had to be sorted so I went to see Tecwyn. He did not prescribe anything except a long period of rest and that is exactly what I did. My parents had gone to Portugal to recover with Clunie so I was alone in Wales.

Above Bolton in Lancashire there is a tiny little village called the Last Drop. It isn't really a village but is known as such. In fact, it comprises of a hotel, pub, swimming pool, conference centre and a few shops. It is so popular and so well-known that it has its own signs on the M61. I remembered when I was ten years old, I went downstairs very early one morning because there was a strange man asleep in one of the guest rooms at The Pole and his snoring had woken me up. In the kitchen there was a vast painting propped up against the Welsh dresser. It was of a man standing on a gallows waiting to be hung. He had a tankard of ale pressed to his lips by the hangman and he was sucking out the last drop. At breakfast my father explained that this 'painting' was, in fact, a pub sign and the strange man snoring in the guest room was a young friend of his called Carton Walker who had just bought an old shippon outside Bolton and was going to turn it into a massive leisure complex, the Last Drop Village.

Carton had married a very beautiful BEA stewardess called Kathy and after two kids, a divorce and Carton's death following a nasty road accident in his Rolls-Royce, Kathy wound up in Windsor. She had always remained close to my parents and while I was vegetating in North Wales I used to talk to her on the phone. One night she suggested that I came to stay for a few days. I had not been there for seven years so I was curious to see how it had changed.

Kathy lived in a lovely cottage in Clewer Court on the outskirts of Windsor. The street name rang a bell, I was sure I knew someone else who lived in Clewer Court, Road? Street? Or whatever. Suddenly it dawned on me, *Anton*, my old mate who had buggered off all those years ago to flog timeshare in Portugal. His parents used to live in Clewer Road. I thought he was probably part of some motorway construction by now or in prison. The telephone directory surrendered his parents' exact address so, on Sunday night, I walked round and rang the doorbell. Anton's mother answered the door.

"Hello Rupert, Anton's doing very well."

Although it had been seven years since I had seen any of them she did not seem surprised to see me. It was as though they had almost expected me to turn up. I was welcomed with open arms and Anton's sister, Sue, got straight on the phone.

"Anton? Guess who has just turned up?"

"Rupert?"

"Yes."

Five minutes later Anton arrived in a black, top-of-the-range BMW and a lot less hair. He gave me an enormous bear hug and said he knew that I would turn up after he had read Julian's obituary in the *Independent*. We went back to his house in St. Leonard's Hill where I met the voluptuous Vanessa who went to bed allowing Anton and I to spend the next five hours swapping stories. Since our last meeting in Portugal he had built up a substantial timeshare property development and, as his mother had so succinctly put it, 'done very well'.

Over the next few weeks I spent a lot of time with Anton in Windsor, and after dinner one night, he asked me if I would be interested in helping him look after the timeshare business in Eastern Europe. I had nothing to lose and a few days later he rang me.

"Rupert, I want you to go to Poznan."
"Okay, but where in the fuck is Poznan?"

Chapter Four

So I was off to this place called Poznan somewhere in the middle of Poland in the Eastern Bloc. I knew nothing of Poland except that my late Aunt Jean had fallen in love with a Polish RAF fighter pilot during the Second World War but had been banned from seeing him by her father since the life expectancy of a fighter pilot was measured in weeks. It broke her heart and she took solace in gin which claimed her at only forty-eight. He survived the War.

I was going to be a direct salesman in the timeshare business. Anton was paying for it all, so I thought *what the heck, let's go look at Poland*. On the twenty-fifth of May 1993, my parents dropped me at Anton's office in Camberley on their way to London. I still did not know what was expected and over dinner that evening I quizzed Anton.

"Look Rupert, just go there, meet up with Goran and I'll brief you in more detail once you have settled in." And that was that.

At Heathrow I had to collect my ticket from the ticket office which was closed. Undeterred, I finally found a member of the Polish airline, LOT, who directed me to the correct check-in desk where my ticket was waiting. The flight was smack on time and I arrived at Warsaw Airport at 2:00pm.

Warsaw Airport was brand new and looked spectacular but the only aircraft in view were LOT and, of course, Lufthansa. Once cleared through customs I was met by a young Englishman called Darren who drove me to the office and, as I had a few hours to kill before catching a train to Poznan, I watched a timeshare presentation which I thought was awful. What had I got myself into? Anyway, no going back now. The train departed Warsaw station at exactly 4:30pm and was due to arrive in Poznan at 19:32pm which it did. Not 19:31pm nor 19:33pm but 19:32pm as advertised. This was quite extraordinary to me as trains in the United Kingdom, apart from being filthy, were invariably late.

This train was immaculate as well as punctual, but how could this be in a country that was supposed to be a Third World member? Apparently Stalin used to make unscheduled train journeys in the USSR and if the train was even a minute late he would climb into the driver's cabin and personally execute him on the spot.

The train was old but clean and the dining car was really rather quaint with red table cloths and little lamps on each table. The toilets were portalooesque and, 'end-of-race-meeting-clean'. The sign that told you not to stick your head out of the window was written in Polish, Russian, German and French but not English. My compartment had the old style sliding doors just like the train in the Harry Potter movies and there were seats for six.

Shortly after the train moved out, two stewards entered and handed out a bun and an orange to each passenger which was a nice touch and one that Sir Richard might like to pick up on. In my carriage there were two Poles, a German, an Italian, one Swiss and me. We all made polite conversation during the journey and, as we were pulling into Poznan station the German, who spoke excellent English, leant over to me and said,

"Zis vould not have been possible in 1943!"

Poznan Station was very dark, dreary and damp. The vast dirt grey hall stank of urine and vomit. Drunks littered the concrete concourse and I felt in imminent peril as my tweed jacket attracted the attention of the gangs of vagabonds that seemed to be a permanent fixture at railway stations. As one group moved towards me I hurried for the exit praying that my contact would be waiting for me, but Goran was nowhere to be seen.

With no idea of where I was going to be staying I had little alternative than to wait so I parked myself right in front of the main entrance. I thought it unlikely that I would be attacked there and the moment I sat down the group moved on.

Goran eventually turned up an hour later and took me to Hotel Poznan, which was to be my home until I found suitable accommodation. After I had checked in he dropped me off at the local Chinese restaurant and left me there.

"Hey Goran! Where are you going?" I demanded, "Anton told me that you were taking me out for dinner."

"I can't. Bojana demands that I come home every night for my evening meal. I'll see you in the morning." What a little wimp. I could not wait to meet Bojana. Despite this unconvincing start to my new life I had a surprisingly good beef and black bean sauce and walked back to the hotel.

As it was only 9:00pm I decided to have a nightcap in one of the hotel bars. The very moment I sat down two women seemed to materialise out of nowhere. One was about twenty-five, six foot tall, quite pretty and had legs that went on forever. She was wearing a piece of string for a T-shirt and a mini-skirt that made the normal version look like a full-length ball gown. Her 'friend' was much older, had a face like a box of spanners, obviously had not had a bath for a decade and her mouth was full of metal.

The tall one ran her fingernails across the nape of my neck, put her lips to my right ear and whispered in a heavy Russian accent, "We want to love you in your room."

At that moment the smelly old one squeezed my left knee, smiled and stuck her rather gnarled hand between my legs. I leapt up immediately sending both the women and my beer flying across the marbled floor. This kerfuffle drew the attention of a tall man wearing a cowboy hat and cowboy boots. His eyes were so close together he was almost Cyclopean. He strode over, snarled at the two tarts and then came over to me.

"I very sorry. I give you both. 100US$." Even his generosity on this buy-one-get-one-free deal could not tempt me so I thanked him and made a hasty retreat to the lifts.

After a quite revolting breakfast I found the office, a small room next to the hotel reception. That's when I met the already notorious Bojana. Bojana and Goran were Serbs from Belgrade. They were both twenty-five with Goran resembling Charlie Chaplin without the moustache. He even had that silly walk and the constant cowering expression on his face as though he was about to be hit.

An ageing chimpanzee crossed with a pit bull terrier with an eye-watering excrescence would best describe Bojana. She was terminally ugly and had a temper to match. I was convinced that if I ever saw Goran naked he would be covered in scars and bruises. They both took an instant dislike to me because they thought Anton had sent me to spy on them which he had. And I did.

'Holiday Club' was the name of the timeshare franchise we were operating out of Hotel Poznan. Anton had built hundreds of luxury apartments in southern Spain and we were going to sell these as timeshares to the Poles. Apart from the terrible two and me, we were *blessed* with other members of staff.

Marta, our translator, was a very beautiful twenty-year old Elizabeth Taylor clone. Her beauty was only exceeded by her dullness and her inability to do anything other than translate.

Malgorzata was our diminutive gofer who ran around all day like a mouse in a maze, achieving precious little and chattering incessantly.

Finally there was Simon, our English bookkeeper and my saviour. He was the only person capable of raising a smile out of Bojana. In addition to the office staff we also had the presentation team which comprised of unreliable Polish sales reps, telephone canvassers and translators.

The telephone canvassers' job was to ring up married couples, conduct a survey about exotic holidays and entice them to a presentation in Hotel Poznan with a gift of a free flight to any European City. On arrival they would be met by one of the Polish reps who would take them to a table, offer them some coffee and, with the aid of a fancy brochure, get their holiday juices flowing.

After about twenty minutes either Bojana or Goran would arrive and start babbling on about the benefits of timeshare ownership. This was very exciting time for the Poles because it was only a few years since the collapse of the Berlin Wall and, although many were starting to make money in new business ventures, very few had actually been anywhere outside of Poland. At the end of the presentation Bojana, Goran and I would go and talk to interested parties and offer them a 20% discount if they signed up there and then.

If they did they had to pay a small deposit on the night, twenty-five percent deposit in the morning, and the full balance within seven days. Business was brisk and, since there were no cheques, credit cards or finance available, all payments were in cash. What funny stuff it was.

On arrival in Warsaw I changed fifty pounds sterling and in return the airport bank cashier gave me one million three hundred thousand zloty. The exchange rate was 26,000 zloty to the pound. Today the currency is still the zloty but they have cut off four zeros. However, back then, it was like playing with monopoly money. The largest note was 2,000,000. The next was: 1,000,000; 500,000; 100,000; 50,000; 20,000; 10,000; 5,000; 1,000; 500; 100 and finally a 50 zloty note which was worth one fifth of one pence.

To make matters worse all the notes were the same size and I was constantly being diddled. After a particularly disgusting dinner in a pizza restaurant I tried to make a complaint but was completely ignored. Requesting the bill had the same effect, so I went in search of my waiter and found him smoking outside. An arguement ensued so when the bill, which was only 196,000 zloty, finally arrived I made it abundantly clear that I expected my 4000 zloty (15p) change in full. They had the last laugh however by handing over eighty 50 zloty notes.

My major problem was communication with the Poles. Polish was, for me anyway, totally unpronounceable. They have four 'Zs' in the alphabet and their word for a rat is '*SZCZUR*'. Apart from the pronunciation problem I was also lazy, had no gift for languages and the Poles only wanted to speak English. The only time they would let you speak Polish is when they asked you to say, '*W Strzebrzeszynie chrzaszcz brzmi w trzcinie i Strzebrzeszyn z tego slynie*', an impossible Polish tongue-twister.

Hotel Poznan was started in the late sixties and completed in the early seventies. It was a vast concrete eyesore in the middle of Poznan but a five minute walk from the Old Market Square. The hotel had sixteen floors, two bars, a disco, numerous shops, a health spa, a cafeteria, numerous offices and a large uninviting communist style dining room.

My room was on the sixteenth floor and had spectacular views of the whole of Poznan. My bed was very comfortable with large square pillows and the room had an en suite avocado coloured bathroom. The hotel towels were tiny and a bit like trying to dry oneself with a piece of coarse-grained sandpaper. The colour television in the corner had a few Polish channels, German channels (of course) and MTV. All films in English were heavily dubbed but it did not matter who was talking in the movie, a man, a woman, a girl or a boy the voice-over was the same and sounded just like a Wagnerian bass.

There were two very sleazy dark bars in the hotel: one opposite the main entrance and one tucked away on the first floor. The downstairs bar was a sunken one. It was very long and had fifteen low, leather-backed swivel seats, equally interspaced along the front. In the corners of the bar were low black leather sofas that once you sat down in one was like being swallowed by a whirlpool. The bar on the first floor was exactly the same design but was not sunken and had swivel seats of a decent height. Both bars closed at 10:00pm; a bit odd for a hotel.

The restaurant was vast. It had an old crimson carpet, brown walls and five huge chandeliers dripped from the ceiling. Each one looked like a thousand empty jam jars had been glued together in a higgledy-piggledy fashion. The waiters were a law unto themselves. When the restaurant was packed you could not find one and when it was empty they were all over the place and, just like all the hotel staff, they had not been taught to smile.

They were still state controlled so, as long as they turned up for work on time, they could not lose their jobs and were paid a bag of apples for their troubles. Matters were not helped by the fact that most of the clientele were fat, beer swilling German businessmen whose only method of communication was to click their fingers at these poor hapless creatures. The irony was that these *suits* were there to help rebuild the Poland that their own fathers had destroyed fifty-five years earlier. The Poles could not stand them. This was not entirely true as there was a certain group that did not exactly like them but needed them.

The ladies who had offered to 'love me in my room' on my first night in Poznan had plenty of colleagues. In the afternoon they would start arriving in the hotel and go straight to the downstairs bar where they would sit in a swivel seat and wait. They came in all shapes and sizes. Many, dropped off by their husbands, quickly removed their wedding rings once inside the foyer.

On one occasion a good looking, middle-aged woman arrived with, what must have been her twin daughters as the family resemblance was striking. These young girls were very pretty and wore short red leather miniskirts, stockings and high heels. Their blouses were cut low and I could see that they had lovely tits. The mother then proceeded to instruct them how to sit, how to pout and how to sip their alcohol free Malibu's. These two girls could have been no more than eighteen years old and their own mother was putting them at the mercy of sweaty, fat lounge lizards.

Well it must have been quite tempting, after all necessity *is* the mother of invention. If you have an unemployed or unemployable husband due to alcoholism, no dole to speak of (£25 per month and bloody difficult to get) and two, poorly educated, pretty girls sitting at home doing nothing, then perching on expense account hotel guests or anyone else for that matter for $100 per hour makes cracking good business sense; lots of them did it.

So from four in the afternoon until the bars closed at ten in the evening there would be a steady stream of punters taking the girls up to their rooms for some light entertainment and then returning them to the bars for more of the same. I could see all of this from our office so even if business was quiet there was never a dull moment. On one day the same girl had five customers in less than two hours. When the bars closed the girls that were left made their way downstairs to the disco. It was free for them but for everyone else there was a small entrance fee of 100,000 zloty.

The disco was awful and the same design as the upstairs bars. More girls would arrive to cater for the hotel guests returning after their dinner engagements. It was like an International Shag Fest conference and the hotel loved it; the manager was getting his cut. Any girl who tried to avoid paying her 'hotel tax' would find herself out on the street. Not any old tart could 'work' Hotel Poznan.

One night, after few beers in the town centre, Simon and I popped in the disco. It was wall to wall prostitutes and businessmen so we made a beeline for the bar and ordered some drinks. We were immediately targeted by a couple of Russian girls who wanted to 'love us in our rooms' but we politely declined and carried on drinking. The disco closed at 3:00am and by that time we were both absolutely plastered and staggered off to our rooms. No sooner had I stumbled into my room than there was a knock at the door. I thought it must be Simon who had probably lost his key and so I opened the door. This Russian girl, who I had refused earlier, barged her way past me, ran into the bathroom and locked the door.

I was sobering up very quickly thinking that her pimp might arrive and beat me up or nick my money or both. A few minutes later she opened the bathroom door, ran out naked, jumped into bed, unwrapped a condom and said:

"For you only fifty dollars."

"Listen to me you fucking bitch get out of my room," and with that I threw her clothes at her. I obviously frightened the shit out of her because she complied immediately.

I was now totally sober and shaking like a leaf and thought that the next day I'd be murdered by some gangland boss but nothing happened and I never saw her working in the hotel again. She had obviously not 'hit' her sales target and been replaced by the latest model. Sometimes it can be a right bugger being in sales. Hit your target and everyone leaves you alone. Miss it and everyone is looking for an excuse to get rid of you.

During the 'Targi Season' all the hotels in Poznan were packed. Targi were Business Fairs and Poznan was the Fair Centre of Poland. Exhibitors came from all over the world and the fairs generally lasted four to five days. All the restaurants, bars, clubs, hotels, toilets and girls doubled their prices. Some of the regular girls in Hotel Poznan were quite pretty but when the fairs were on they shipped in the real professionals, mainly from Moscow. These girls were stunning. Nearly all six foot tall, blond, wore very short black dresses, hold-up stockings and black patent leather high heeled stilettos. Not all of them wore knickers.

There was one girl who worked the hotel on her own and somehow got away with it. Wiktoria was from the Ukraine and spoke adequate English. She wore jeans, T-shirts, no bra and looked just like the girl Julia Roberts portrayed in Pretty Woman, very easy on the eye. She did not work the bars or the disco but used to sit in the cafeteria and spot her prey. Once identified she would pounce. She rarely failed and seemed to work on a two week on, two week off basis. I was fascinated by her and wanted to know more.

All the other girls were run as part of a farm but this one was different and the others must have not minded or did not know about her. I am sure that the pimps would not like it if even one 50 zloty note was diverted from their accounts. So, one day, while she was having her coffee in the cafeteria, I went up and sat at her table.

"What are you doing here? You cannot afford me. Go away!" she barked. Either my snappy suit wasn't so snappy or she had heard about my lack of funds for such activities. I explained that I was only interested in finding out how she managed to work in this snake pit.

"Look, I am nineteen. I am from Zhytomyr in the Ukraine. My parents have no money and I have five younger brothers and they all need feeding. I go home every two weeks with my money and I am saving up to marry my fiancé. I reckon that by the time I am twenty-five I will have enough to stop this filthy business. I hate every minute of it but I have no other way of providing for my family." With that she got up and left.

Judging by the way she used to smile at her quarry I doubt there was one shred of truth in her charming little story.

Chapter Five

The City of Poznan was built on the river Warta and is almost exactly equidistant between Berlin and Warsaw, approximately three hundred kilometers from each city. The site dates back to the tenth century when it was a sentry post on the river where roads from the east to the west and from the north to the south crossed. It is now the main city of the Wielkopolska district and was once the capital of Poland. Over the years Poznan has had a very rough ride. It has been attacked by the Brandenbergs, the Swedes, the Russians, the Prussians and the final act of destruction came at the end of the Second World War when almost every building, especially in the Old Town and Old Market Square was razed to the ground by the Germans.

After the war the Old Market Square was restored completely to its 'former glory'. Stary Rynek, as it is called, is a wreath of charming multi-coloured facades of historic tenements: houses strewn with aristocratic residences. It is dominated by the Town Hall and at noon every day the famous butting goats come out and strut their stuff in front of the vast clock face on top of the Hall. Apart from a quite monstrous communist concrete building next to the Town Hall that was erected in the sixties, Stary Rynek is one of the prettiest town centres I have ever visited.

When I lived there, the population of Poznan was around six hundred thousand, most living in large concrete tower blocks dotted around the city, covering an area twenty kilometers square. There were several beautiful lakes in and around Poznan, the best probably Strzeszynek, impossible to pronounce, but great to swim in. When I first got to Poznan there were two zoos, one with animals and one without, or so it seemed. The zoo with animals was very sad to behold. The lion's mane had all but fallen out, the animal in the tiger's enclosure looked nothing like a tiger and the elephant had only half a tusk. The zoo without animals was, in fact, supposed to be a safari park. The local government, strapped for cash, had only been able to buy a few, and they were in permanent hiding!

On Saturday mornings I used to buy a copy of *The Times*, usually two days old, walk down to Stary Rynek and sit outside my favourite café. During the summer many of the cafes in the square had colourful outside seating platforms and I would sit there for hours, reading my newspaper and watching the world go by. The owner of this particular café only employed tall pretty girls and hot pants were part of their uniform. As a result his café was always full. I did not really read *The Times* but used it as a prop to draw attention to myself. It worked quite well as lots of people used to come over to my table, ask me if I was English, sit down and start chatting away. This way I met loads of different people: Americans, Swedes, Germans, French, other English and, most importantly, Polish girls who always wanted to practice their English.

The most amusing crowd I met at the café were the 'Cigarette Boys'. These were a bunch of British engineers who worked for a very large American cigarette company. They were employed to travel around the world and teach the local employees of this company how to be more cost-effective in the production of cigarettes. They were spending the summer of '93 working at the Mars factory in Poznan. Apart from being a chocolate bar, Mars is also a Polish brand of cigarette.

These troubleshooters were very loud, drank heavily and entertained me enormously. They were all staying in Hotel Mercury, where the sultry Wiktoria now patrolled. I used to hang around with two of them in the main: Allan, who spent all his money on prostitutes, and Davey who was desperate to get into Wiktoria's knickers for as little as possible.

Davey was Scottish, had a broad Glaswegian accent and was affectionately known as 'Hair-Dryer Dave'. He was the spitting image of Barry Manilow and had all the accoutrements: gold bracelets, gold chains round his neck, longish blond permed hair, cream suit, a deep orange tan and beige crocodile shoes.

One Friday evening Davey came bouncing into the café in a very ebullient mood.

"Right Rupert, mine's a large one please. I've just hit the fucking jackpot."

"What, you've finally got into Wiktoria's knickers at your price?"

"No you stupid twat! For the first time in twenty years I've made twenty million cigarettes in one day."

Most of the time I met the Cigarette Boys at the café, but one day we stumbled across the best place in Poznan - The Green Pub. This was in the basement of an old apartment block just off Sw Marcin Street, very close to Stary Rynek. The three rich little old ladies who owned the building had seen there was a need for Irish beer in Poznan so they opened a bar and imported draught Guinness and Kilkenny directly from Dublin. It was run by one of their grandsons, Pawel and his friend Roman. The Guinness was perfect but expensive for Poland, about £1.20 a pint.

The pub also had a dart board which the Poles had never seen before. Their idea of how to play darts was to stand about twenty feet from the board and throw the darts as hard as they possible could in the general direction of the board. This was bloody dangerous as they never hit the board and darts would ricochet of the walls and land in peoples drinks. On the occasion that one dart embedded itself in someone's head we felt that it was time to teach the Poles how to play.

This proved to be an excellent move as the female students thought it was a quaint little game and were queuing up to learn. One night I was playing darts with Allen and a couple of gorgeous girls came into the pub. Like all the others they were fascinated by this English pub game and begged to play. After a few pints of Guinness they asked us if we would like to escort them to the student disco, Trops, on the university campus. The disco was one huge room. A bar at one end with some beaten up old tables and benches for seats and the DJ and dance floor at the other end.

The bar only served Lech beer but it was cheap and the music was great dance music but a trifle loud for a thirty-four year old. All the boys were in the bar getting pissed and all the girls were dancing. This was definitely heaven. Beer and about two hundred lovely girls.

Occasionally we could be found in Palladium. This was the poshest club in town, frequented by the Poznan Mafia and their whores. On Allan's birthday all the other Cigarette Boys and I went out for dinner and then on to Palladium. At about three in the morning most of them had left leaving me and Davey still sitting at the bar. After one more drink Davey went outside to organise a taxi. No sooner had he left than one of the remaining tarts sat next to me and asked me to buy her a drink. I refused and she glanced across the club towards a table where some large hoods were sitting. In a second, one of them came over, grabbed me by the arm and said in very broken English;

"*Vot iz vrong viz mi zizter*?"

Being a bit drunk I decided to take this bruiser on.

"Look mate, nothing. She fucking gorgeous but, if she's your sister, I suggest you take her home and put her to bed okay? And what's more I want my bloody arm back," and with that I wrenched my arm from his grip. I am not sure if he understood what I had said but my aggressive stance seemed to have worked as he transferred his grip from my arm to hers and dragged her back to the mob in the corner. Davey felt I had been rather fortunate.

Trops was the 'people's disco' and Palladium was the corporate toilet. In between the two we swiftly found Studio Jacks which, despite its reputation of being the most dangerous, was the most fun by a country mile. Downstairs was a huge pool and snooker hall which was always full of young Poznanians and upstairs was the nightclub. The pool part was free but the entrance fee to the nightclub was 100,000 zloty. The disco was excellent and the dance floor was surrounded by low tables and huge deep leather sofas. There was a bar at the end and television screens everywhere playing the videos to the dance music. The bar staff all wore uniforms and all had a badge saying BARMAN, irrespective of their gender. Jacks was packed nearly every night and there were always a few tables reserved for the hoods and their girls. These girls used to dance round their hand bags hoping to attract the right customer while the hoods would monitor their progress while swigging Chivas Regal whisky from the bottle.

If you wanted to dance with one of the girls she would check first with '*The Table*' and, if she got the nod, then you could, but if she did not, then leaving immediately was the best course of action. We learned very early on that this was a no-go area so we never got involved and, as a result, were left alone.

One poor lonely rather drunk Dutchman fancied his chances with one of the girls but, instead of retreating when his advances were rebuffed, he put his arms round her and tried to kiss her. One of the hoods picked up a glass ashtray, jumped onto the dance floor and smashed it over his head. He crumpled to the ground in a pool of blood with a huge hole in his head. Nobody moved a muscle and this sad soul was picked up by two other hoods, taken downstairs and thrown out into the street. The floor was quickly cleaned and everyone, including us, carried on as though nothing had happened.

I was beginning to make a bit of money at work so it was time to look for alternative accommodation. I moved into a very basic, but fully furnished two bedroom apartment on the third floor of the Osiedle Tysiaclecia housing estate.

One day, due to a power cut, the afternoon presentation was cancelled so I went home. When I got there I found my landlady, dressed in stuff you would only find in a sex shop, entertaining two oriental gentlemen. I later discovered that she had nowhere to live and had been dossing with friends. She used the flat to take baths and host sex parties on a regular basis. As this was a two bedroom apartment, I suggested that she halved my rent and moved into the second room which she gratefully did. From that moment on there was never any problem, but I had to put a stop to her clients staying the night; they tended to dominate the bathroom in the mornings.

From about the age of four I used to stand on a stool and watch Shuffy cook. I had also picked up a few culinary skills from my father, who was an excellent, naturally gifted chef, having honed his mastery with whale meat during the war. Now that I was out of Hotel Poznan and liberated from disgusting hotel food, I was able to go to the local markets and buy my own produce. Each housing estate had its own market selling everything from hunks of pork to underpants. The vegetables were fantastic but my favourite shops were the butchers. They had the most delicious range of hams and sausages I had ever seen, and I decided that if I ever got on *Desert Island Discs* my luxury, without any hesitation, would be biala kielbasa, white sausage.

There seemed to be a chemist on every corner and a dentist on every other and there was a plethora of shoe and lingerie shops. I understood the presence of these shops but

I never saw the reason for so many chemists and dentists. I considered the reason and came up with the combination of drinking too much Polish vodka would give you a headache and potentially make your teeth fall out. Apart from the vodka and beer there was nothing else much to drink. It was possible to buy wine but it was pretty filthy and mainly came from Bulgaria. French champagne, wine and Johnny Walker whisky were available in some city centre outlets but were exorbitantly expensive.

Travelling around Poznan was easy; plenty of very cheap taxis, even cheaper buses and dangerous trams. Taxis were great for short journeys and buses and trams for longer ones. My first time on a bus I noticed that there was no conductor. How was I to buy a ticket? As others got on they inserted little green oblong bits of paper into a small paper-punching device which was fastened to the inside of the bus on a pole by the folding doors. I asked an old lady where I could by a ticket but she didn't understand me. At the next stop three burly looking men got on. They were unshaven and all wore bobble hats but without the bobble and started moving up and down the bus checking people's tickets. When they got to me I tried to buy a ticket.

"Deutsch?" One of them enquired.

"No. I am English." And pulled out my passport. At that moment the bus made another stop and the three men bundled me off the bus. They started flicking through my passport and growled at me. Finally, one of them started babbling at me in Polish. He then wrote down on a piece of paper 150,000 zloty and waved it in front of my face. I didn't have a bean on me, so they arrested me. I was frogmarched down the road to the local police station and locked in a cell. Two hours later a uniformed policeman came into my cell but there was no sign of the three bobble hatted bruisers. This time PC Plod gave me a piece of paper with 500,000 zloty written on it. The price on my head had tripled. When it finally dawned on him that I *really* had no money and that he had no immediate way of extracting any from me, he shrugged his shoulders, gave my passport back and pointed to the exit.

Taxis in Poznan were usually old Audis, Mercedes or Volkswagens and incredibly cheap compared to London cabs. You could travel around Poznan for the equivalent of a few quid as long as you got into a regulated radio cab. There were, however, plenty of bandit cabs, sometimes indistinguishable from radio ones. In addition they would come up with any excuse or idea, however preposterous, to load the fee. From my flat to Hotel Poznan cost 50,000 zloty but one day my usual cabby was not at the taxi rank and in his place was a bandit. I had no option but to take the bandit and tried to settle the price before we left. He ignored me and when we arrived the meter showed 200,000 zloty, four times the normal price. So armed with my 'communication pad' and pen I scribbled down the normal fee.

"You Engleeze. You smoke in taxi. You pay extra," he explained but this was bollocks. No way was I going to pay. I gave him 50,000 zloty, got out and gave him a middle finger for good measure. Filled with rage and screaming obscenities he jumped out of his taxi and took a swing at me with a wheel spanner. He missed. The hotel security leaped on top of him and shortly after he was carted away by the police. His car was driven to the far end of the underground car park where it stayed for months.

As there were very few domestic telephones in Poland calling for a cab was not an option so you just had to walk to the nearest taxi rank and hope. I thought about buying a car but for the cost of a car I could travel every day in Poznan by taxi for a year and a half and I did not see myself spending that much time in Poland.

There were public telephones all over the place but ninety-nine percent had been vandalised. The phones also required special tokens as there were no coins in the Polish monetary system. These tokens could only be bought from the Post Office which was either shut or overflowing with customers and the queues sometimes went right round the block. Our office had three lines and one was always broken. Local calls presented no problems but any international calls could take hours to get through and, when you eventually did, you were invariably cut-off.

We employed a contract typist called Hanka. She was the lady who dealt with all the paperwork once a timeshare week had been sold. She was about forty-five years old, married and had two kids. One morning she came rushing into the office, flung her arms around my neck, gave me a huge fat kiss on the cheeks and started shrieking with delight.

"I've got a telephone! I've got a telephone! I've got a telephone!"

"Calm down Hanka, so you got a telephone, great. Now will you please get on with your work, you are already half an hour late this morning." She would not sit still for a minute and suddenly picked up the phone and started dialing a number.

"Hanka, who are you ringing?" I asked.

"I'm ringing me." she replied, grinning from ear to ear.

"What do you mean you're ringing you? You're here!"

"I know but I just wanted to see if my phone works."

"Does it?" I asked.

"Yes, yes, it does." She said excitedly.

"Wonderful. I am very pleased for you; now can you get on with some work?" She put the receiver down and I left to buy some cigarettes. When I came back she was back on the phone again ringing herself and this continued throughout the entire day until she finished at 6:00pm. I later found out that she and her husband had put their names on a list to have a telephone installed and it had finally arrived, eighteen years later.

I was really beginning to enjoy myself for the first time in years: the pain of Jules' death was receding; I was making a bit of money; had a nice apartment and was being kept amused by the Cigarette Boys. One Saturday I invited Davey and Allan round for dinner and suggested that they arrived early so we could go to the local 'Drink Bar' for an aperitif. The old Polish 'Drink Bars' were just that, a bare room at the end of a mini-market where you could get a drink. They served all different types of vodka and a few Polish beers, usually Lech Pils and EB. The bars were always very dark, smelly and had little furniture but the booze was cheap. It was a nice evening so Marek, the manager of my local Drink Bar, had put some plastic tables and chairs outside. We ordered some beers and started a conversation about the Polish drinking habits.

We agreed that: when a New Zealand baby boy is born the first thing it picks up is a rugby ball; an English baby boy a cricket bat; and judging by the number of drunks about, the Polish baby boy, a vodka bottle. The Polish men took their vodka very seriously and always drank it straight. Sometimes they would chase it down with fresh orange juice or beer, but if a Pole tells you he's not had a drink for ten days, what he means is that he has not had any *vodka* for ten days.

Vodka is not a Russian invention. In fact the earliest sign of vodka was in Poland in the eighth century and it was a crude spirit made by freezing wine. The initial use for vodka was as a medicine and, believe it or not, an aftershave. Pablo Picasso once said, "The three most astonishing things in the past half century were the Blues, Cubism and Polish Vodka."

It was very easy to tell when it was payday in Poznan because there was always a long queue at the alcohol counters of every single mini-market. These thirsty men would spend their meagre wages on bottles of vodka, drink the entire contents and then pass out. On Thursdays, Fridays and Saturdays there would be bodies littered all over the place and, over the course of Saturday, they would start sobering up and then go round begging for more money for more booze. Not every male in Poland behaved like this, in fact precious few, but it was, nevertheless, a very serious problem; dead-end jobs, wife on the game, very little money and cheap booze.

It was not just confined to Poland. All the former Soviet bloc countries suffered to some degree and Russia itself was probably the worst case. I remember talking to some expert on the Russian armed forces while I was stationed in Germany. His argument was that we should not have spent billions on our nuclear deterrent as fighting the Russians could be like poaching pheasants. Fill a shoe polish tin top full of grain soaked in vodka, and you could walk round the next morning and just pick them up, marinated to boot. Apart from the alcoholism within the ranks of the Russian army there was also a huge language problem. It was not rare to find five different languages spoken in a Company of one hundred and twenty soldiers. This is where the expression 'drunk and disorderly' must have come from. One could argue that booze is the reason why we have not yet had a Third World War; too pissed to press the red button.

I was cooking a haunch of pork for dinner which was going to take ages so we had time for another drink. As our beers arrived so did 'Green T-Shirt'. Green T-Shirt was about thirty but looked sixty. He was short and very thin. His head resembled a dried out old conker that had been left roasting in the oven for too long. Greasy brown hair was matted to his scalp and his eyes were like tiny red shiny rubies that had been pushed into a brown bun so you could only just see them.

He was known as 'Green T-Shirt' as he never wore anything else. To accompany this he also wore a filthy, chocolate brown suit. He spent most of his days hovering between the Drink Bar and the off-license in the mini-market. When anyone left the Drink Bar he would scurry along and hoover up any drops left in the glasses and empty the ash trays into his pockets in the hope of finding a smoke-able dog-end. He was such a pathetic sight that a passer-by would pity him and give him money and, once he had enough for a miniature bottle of Premium vodka, he was off to the boozer. Desperate for business there was no question of the licensee adopting a 'Drink Aware' policy.

Once he'd controlled his shaking hands just enough so he could open the screw top bottle, he would then vacuum suck every last drop before staggering outside. Another source of income was empty beer bottles. Every morning you could see the likes of GTS rummaging around the communal bin areas searching for undamaged beer bottles which could be returned for a few zloty.

That evening GTS hit the jackpot as some stupid fool had given him enough money for half a litre of vodka. The alcohol hit as he left the shop. He lurched forward sharply. His target was a lamp-post but his outstretched arms passed either side and his head smashed side-on into the post. With blood dripping from his nose he slid helplessly to the ground and rolled over onto his back. He lay there motionless for about five minutes. Davey and Allan thought he was dead but I assured them that this was his daily routine. A dark patch started to appear in the region of his crotch and a few seconds later the entire top half of his trousers had turned a darker shade of brown. He suddenly sat up, looked at his crutch, grimaced and then, with the help of the lamp-post, pulled himself to his feet. He steadied himself against the post and after a few minutes he looked pretty firm on his feet. First he let go of the post with his right hand, then with his left hand and finally he tried to walk - big mistake. He took one step, lost his balance completely and managed to grab hold of the post just in time to stop himself crashing to the ground again. This went on for about twenty minutes and each time he tried to walk the result was the same. Eventually he gave up trying to walk and decided to clean up his bloodied nose. Holding onto the lamp-post with one arm he put the other hand into his urine-stained trouser pocket and pulled out a disgusting looking snot-encrusted handkerchief and started blowing his nose.

What he hadn't noticed was, that when he had pulled out his handkerchief, he had also released a few low denomination zloty notes which were now lying on the grass a few feet away. When he saw the cash, panic gripped him and he made a desperate dive towards the money but missed by a mile. The draught caused by the down force of his body blew the money further away so he lay there pondering on what to do next. After several minutes he made it onto all fours and slowly started to crawl towards his cash but when he had just about got there a sudden gust of wind blew it even further away. His knees and arms crumpled beneath him and he was back to square one.

However, GTS was not to be beaten. He somehow regained his strength, got back onto all fours and slowly but surely reduced the distance between himself and the deposit on his next miniature. Soon it was all safely back in his trouser pocket. We had been watching all of this from only a few yards away and not once did it cross our minds to help. In the end he did not need any and quite soon afterwards he was on his feet again ready to face the world.

Chapter Six

It was late June 1993 and the 'Cigarette Boys' work at the Mars factory had run its course. Their next assignment was in Brasov, an industrial city in Romania. Allan did not want to go, as he had fallen in love with one of the hookers, but Davey reminded him that he always fell in love with hookers. I was going to miss them and when Simon suddenly resigned because he just could not stand Bojana any longer, I felt a bit deflated. Bojana took over the accounts but made a pig's ear of things. For a start she was not sending enough of the money back to the UK to pay for the timeshare weeks and so Anton, much to Bojana's annoyance, installed Nigel as our new bookkeeper.

Nigel did not have hair. Instead he had a thick coarse brown carpet on his head. He was about five foot tall, rotund and wore thick steel-rimmed glasses. He was quite the opposite of Simon. He did not drink, he rarely spoke, he ate alone, he arrived for work at 9:00am and left at 5:00pm in a rather Stalinesque manner. He was, fundamentally, a crashing bore. He had no redeeming features whatsoever and reminded me of one of those people who continually set themselves staggeringly low targets and consistently fail to achieve them.

Since Davey and Allan had left I had not ventured out, so one day I invited our new *accountant* from London to dinner. He refused at first, but once I had explained that at '*Chez Miller*' he was going to get food to eat instead of the hotel slop they dished up every night, he changed his mind. After work we went back to my flat via the local market to pick up some grub and then onto Marek's Drink Bar for a libation. Silly me, Nigel did not drink. This was a lie. He actually did; he drank like a waste disposal unit but did not want the Serbs to know as he had heard them complaining about my partying with Simon and the Cigarette Boys. Once again it was a lovely evening and so we sat outside the bar and had a few beers. GTS turned up looking remarkably fresh, walking without any aids, so I gave him a cigarette.

The white sausages were delectable and, once Nigel had been lubricated with Polish beer, he became quite chatty. Unfortunately all he wanted to talk about was cars, a subject that had always been alien to me. The only way to stop his interminable droning on about the UK car industry was to drag him into town. We jumped in a taxi and 50,000 zloty later were in Stary Rynek. We walked round this majestic square with all the brightly lit cafes filling up quickly and then I saw her. My legs suddenly crumpled like a Fred Dibnah chimney stack and I had to sit down immediately.

She had masses of fuzzy, strawberry blond hair, big, big, beautiful blue eyes and the most enchanting smile I had ever seen. I was instantly in love, totally smitten in one second flat. My heart was beating so fast it almost blew up and I was shaking like a leaf. Nigel thought I was having a heart attack. She was sitting in the next café to us and another girl was sitting beside her. They seemed to be engrossed in a conversation with a young man who was sitting opposite them and with his back facing us. She glanced up at me, smiled and then carried on her conversation. That did it. I wanted that girl. She was going to be mine.

At that very moment I decided that I was going to spend the rest of my life with her. No question about it. The deal was done. All I had to do now was to make sure it happened. This was not going to be easy. After all, the young man with her was more than likely her boyfriend, fiancé or even husband, so I stood no chance unless I murdered him but there was no future in that for either of us. My plans were bolstered to some degree when she kept on stealing glances at me that I never missed. How could I? I could not take my eyes off her. I was so excited and the thought that I might actually soon be talking to her sent me into a state of delicious freefall.

The moment had arrived. I had to go and talk to her. I drank my beer, girded my loins and was just about to make the decisive move when the doubts started to arrive. What was I going to say and how? I did not speak any Polish and I doubted if she spoke English. What if the man with them started a fight? What if she wasn't looking at me but the bloke behind me? The negatives were pouring in by the container load and I hesitated, ordered another beer, sat down and lit another cigarette. I was pondering on my next move while blowing smoke rings in her general direction when suddenly the three of them got up and left. What a catastrophe! Rupert you fool, you've blown it. I said to myself. They headed across the cobbled square and by the time old Cowardly Custard had weighed up all the options the three of them had disappeared forever.

"Rupert? Why did you not go after that girl?" Nigel quizzed.

"Err…. What girl Nigel?"

"The girl you have been staring at for the last thirty minutes and who has been staring back at you."

"Was it that obvious?"

"Yes!"

Nigel got up and went for a piss. I lit yet another cigarette, smoked it and Nigel still had not returned so I thought I better go and look for him. I stood up, turned round and there she was striding towards me, grinning from ear to ear. Nigel and her friend were a few yards behind her and there was no sign of the man they were with. She stopped about a yard in front of me and stuck out her hand. I took it in mine and I was off to the moon, the stars and beyond.

"Hi, my name is Rupert. What is yours?"

"Katarzyna."

The four of us sat down, ordered some drinks and started chatting. Well that's not quite true. I sat opposite Katarzyna and Nigel sat opposite her friend, Justyna. Justyna spoke a little English and Nigel, I discovered, spoke a little Polish as it turned out that his ex-wife was Polish. Katarzyna's English was limited and I spoke no Polish but it did not matter. We both stuck our heads in our hands and stared at each other for about an hour.

Justyna started to make those, 'I want to go home' noises, but I was having none of that crap so I suggested, by doing my air shot impression of Jimmy White playing snooker, that we all go and play pool in Studio Jacks. Katarzyna grabbed Justyna, pulled her to one side and judging by her mannerisms was probably advising her friend that if she did not come she would break her neck.

Jacks was reasonably quiet as it was early on a Tuesday night. We found a pool table and I teamed up with Katarzyna to play Nigel and Justyna. Katarzyna was clueless which gave me the opportunity to wrap my arms round her on the premise that I was teaching her how to hold the cue properly. After one game we went dancing upstairs. I pulled her on to the dance floor and in a matter of seconds we were kissing passionately. I could not believe it and nor could Justyna. She was absolutely flabbergasted. She had never seen her best friend behave in such a wanton manner before.

Nigel and Justyna sat and talked and we just snogged all night. At 5:00am Jacks closed and we took the girls back to Justyna's parents' house by taxi. Using my best sign language and a little of her English I did my best to ask her if we could meet at the same café what had now become later that day. I was not one hundred percent sure of her answer but I convinced myself it was a definite 'yes'.

On the way back to my flat via Hotel Poznan Nigel explained me why he had been so long in the loo at the café. He had walked in to the 'ladies' by mistake only to find Katarzyna and Justyna hanging around. Katarzyna had wanted to meet me but could not do it while this man, a drunk student, was sniffing after Justyna. She persuaded her to leave the café, knowing the man would follow. This duly happened and they managed to lose him. She then persuaded Justyna to come back to the café to meet up with us. However, how could they do this without appearing too forward? That's how they ended up in the 'ladies' and when Nigel told Katarzyna that I was crazy about her then all the barriers were lifted and she felt she could put her cards very firmly on the table. Thank god she did and that is how I met the very, very beautiful Katarzyna Przybyszewska.

I got back to my flat at about six-thirty in the morning. The sun was getting out of bed and it was going to be another lovely day in every sense. I slept for a couple of hours and then went to work. It was the longest day ever and the hours just crawled by. My mind was totally focused on my evening rendezvous with Katarzyna at the café. Fortunately business was quiet so I could sit there and dream about her while reminding myself that there was no chance of her turning up.

As my luck would have it a storm started brewing near Poznan and by 7:00pm the rain was sheeting down and the roads had turned into rivers. No way was she going to show in this weather and I had no idea where she lived. I was punctual and ordered a beer. 8:00pm came and went and so did the next half hour. I was about to leave when it suddenly stopped raining and I had this strange warm feeling flow through my entire body. Just wait Rupert, I thought, she is going to show.

Five minutes later this spellbindingly beautiful creature walked in the cafe. She was wearing a pretty white dress with blue flowers on it and far too much red lipstick. It was an awkward second meeting. I wanted to kiss her on the lips and she just wanted a peck on the cheek. Our faces collided into each other with the net result that neither of us got the expected kiss and I ended up with red lipstick all over my chin. We sat down in one of the booths at the back of the café, looked at each other nervously and wandered what to do next.

"Would you like a drink?" I offered, gesturing with my right hand.

"Kawa prosze."

She sipped her coffee and I drank my beer and we just smiled gently at each other. I knew how old I was and she knew how old she was. The problem was how were we going to tell each other and when we found out was that going to be that? She pulled a piece of paper and a pen from her hand bag and started to show me that by adding certain numbers together you could determine someone's age. *You sneaky swine*, I thought; *you clever little gorgeous sexy devil*. I pretended not to understand what on earth she was up to and after about half an hour I thought let's just get this over with and hope for the best.

"How old do you think I am?" She looked at me, grimaced and said rather hopefully,

"Twenty-five…?"

"No."

"Twenty-eight….?"

"No. I'm thirty-four, married but getting divorced." Lots of sign language was required to make sure she fully understood my situation which she did. What chance had I of her believing me? I mean, how many pretty girls have been told by men that they are getting divorced?

Her jaw hit the table, her eyes popped out on stalks and her hands were shaking so much she couldn't pick up her coffee. Well that was bound to be the end of another beautiful relationship and I just waited for her to thank me for the coffee and leave. She probably wouldn't even do that and I half expected her just to leg it. She didn't. She just sat there and stared at me. After about ten minutes she said, "How old do you think I am?"

"Twenty?"

Well I was a year out. She was nineteen. Wow! There I was sitting in a café in Poznan with the most gorgeous girl in the whole world who I had fallen deeply in love with. She was Polish, nineteen years old and Catholic. I was thirty-four, English, married, of no religious persuasion of any description, and we did not speak the same language. This show was going to run and run!

I suddenly had a good idea. I'll tell her a joke. The question was could I find a funny joke that could be easily told without speaking Polish. With the aid of a pen, a few beer mats, lots of arm waving and some charade like acting, I began. There was this man on a train who was desperate for a shit so he leaves his compartment and goes to the loo. The first loo he finds is occupied so he goes to the next one and this too is occupied. The third loo is closed for repairs and there isn't a fourth as, by now, he's come to the end of the train. Not only that but he has become desperate and is having to cross his legs and shuffle back down the corridor to prevent an accident in his trousers. By sheer luck he comes across an empty compartment, enters and closes the door behind him. He manages to draw the door blinds, shuffles across the compartment and opens the window. He quickly takes his trousers and pants off, stands with one foot on either seat and sticks his bare bum out of the window. At that very moment the train approaches a tunnel and the guard at the rear of the train sticks his head out of a window and screams;

"We are approaching a tunnel. All heads in, all heads in please; including the man with the big cigar!" Katarzyna shrieked with laughter and the ice was broken. With the help of two pens, lots of props and much arm waving we chatted away like long lost friends for hours. When the supply of beer mats was finally exhausted we went dancing until dawn.

On my return to the flat I found a note from my landlady saying that I would have to vacate the premises immediately as her father had been kicked out of the marital home by her mother and was moving in today. She was not around to discuss the matter so I packed my belongings and moved back to Hotel Poznan.

Katarzyna and I spent the next ten days sitting in cafes, communicating with her little English and me writing on beer mats, snogging and dancing until daybreak. One night we agreed to meet at Studio Jacks much later as she had some family matters to attend to first. As usual she was late and had arrived in tears.

"I can't see you anymore," she announced, "I have friends waiting in a car outside and we are going to a party. Goodbye." She turned and started to leave. Well I should not have been surprised. Can you imagine her family's reaction?

"Hi mum. Guess what? You know my lovely, good looking, twenty-three year old boyfriend called Adam, whose parents are well off, god fearing and church attending Catholics just like us and who everyone thinks I will eventually marry. Well I've dumped him, because I have fallen in love with a tall thirty-four year old Englishman. He is a little tubby, has no money, drinks, smokes, borders on atheism and is married but tells me he is in the process of getting a divorce, but his lovely face and blue eyes knock the spots of Adam."

"YOU ARE NEVER TO SEE THAT MAN EVER AGAIN. IS THAT PERFECTLY UNDERSTOOD KATARZYNA?"

She did, however, have the decency to come and tell me in person.

As she was leaving Jacks I grabbed her by the arm and pleaded with her.

"Look, has the last ten days meant nothing to you? Please just spend half an hour with me. Okay?"

"No. Let me go. My friends are waiting."

"Ten minutes….Please."

"Well……..alright, but only ten." With that she ran out and told her friends, which included the doomed Adam, to go ahead and she'd follow shortly. At 6:00am we ordered breakfast in an old 24 hour café on Sw. Marcin Street.

The next night was a disaster. It nearly ruined everything. As usual we met in our café and ended up in Studio Jacks. After dancing a little we found a dark little corner and I was virtually undressing her. This made her uncomfortable and at about 4:00am she wanted to go home but I persuaded her to come back with me to the hotel. To get to the lifts you have to walk past the reception.

"Mr. Miller. I say Mr. Miller?"

"Yes?"

"Will you please register your lady guest?"

"No, no, you don't understand. She's actually a friend of mine."

"Yes we quite understand Mr. Miller, but all girls must be registered."

This did two things. Firstly, it made me out to look like a serial shagger and secondly, it made her feel like a two bit tart. By the time we got to my room we both felt dreadful. We went to bed, did a bit of meaningless fumbling and fell asleep.

The next morning we went downstairs and the receptionists were giggling at us which made matters worse. Katarzyna hurried off as fast as she could.

"Café tonight?" I called out after her but she did not answer.

After another tasteless dinner at the hotel, I strolled to our café in the vain hope that I might see her again. I took a copy of *The Times* with me as an emotional prop. It was another lovely late June evening and I got to our café at about 8:00pm. I ordered a beer, lit a fag and read my newspaper. From time to time I'd do a quick scan around the square just in case. I had more beers, more fags and had finished reading *The Times* so I thought I'd have a crack at the crossword.

"Last night was a mistake." I looked up and she was standing there looking more beautiful than ever.

"Yes it was," I agreed. "Let's not do that again.... Well not yet." She smiled one of her zapping smiles and sat down. Business as usual or so I thought.

We met again the next night and this time she hit me with a real bomb-shell.

"I'm going to France next week with Justyna for a three month university practical training programme."

"You're joking?"

"No, we are going next Tuesday, hitch-hiking our way to Nice and we start work in Hotel Acropolis. After that we have a year off from our studies so we are going to work our way from Nice to Australia and stay there for a bit."

I blinked several times, gulped and felt like an enemy plane had just shot me down, my cockpit was jammed, my parachute on fire and I was in a tailspin heading for the ground and a certain death. Stay cool. Do not panic, after all three months isn't very long is it? It's fucking ages! And what about this Australian idea? What in the hell was I going to do? All of my plans had just been shredded. This was a crisis far worse than Suez. It was, quite frankly, the end of the world.

"Yeah, you go to France. You'll have a great time. The food is good and you'll meet loads of new people and I'll just stay here ON MY OWN in Poznan." I said in a rather nonchalant manner, hoping she would come to her senses, cancel her plans and stay with me. It was a 'take it away' type of sale. 'You can't afford it, Sir'. It did not work.

"Oh thank god for that," she beamed, "I thought you'd be really upset."

Katarzyna and Justyna packed up and went to Nice.

Life without her was unbearable. I tried dating other girls but try driving a Trabant or a Volga when you've been used to an Aston Martin. I could not stop thinking of her and at night I used to have nightmares where garlic smelling Frenchmen would drool over her. Yuck! What I really wanted to do was go to Nice and drag her back to my cave but I had no money and hitch-hiking was out of the question. Pretty girls can hitch-hike successfully but stale doughnuts cannot.

Before she left she gave me the telephone number of Hotel Acropolis so I rang the hotel and asked them for their fax number. I was going to give her a damn good faxing. Over the next two and a half months, when the Serbs were not in the office, I sent her over forty faxes. At first they were chatty newsletters but later simply said, 'I love you. Come back before I shoot myself!' On her birthday I got a friend of mine in the UK to send her the biggest bunch of flowers he could find and I asked David Rae to send me a Rupert Bear annual. He did with a note. 'I doubt if I am wise sending you this as you probably want to use it to get into some innocent girl's knickers!' How David thought I could use a children's annual, A4 in size, to get into a girl's knickers I do not know. I sent the book, not the note to France. Quite out of the blue I got a fax back. She was quitting her course, shelving Australia and coming home.

We met at our café and talked and kissed and kissed and talked. We went to Jacks and then went back to my new apartment. While Katarzyna had been in France I had moved into a very modest little place in the Poznan district of Lazurowa. I had a bedroom, kitchen, bathroom and a large sitting room. I liked it. It was home. That was the first night we slept together. I asked her to move in with me but she would not.

Although we were madly in love there were still prejudices to deal with and so she used to come and go as she pleased and, as there were no phones, communication was impossible. I assumed that her family had either capitulated or had decided to let her get '*The Englishman*' out of her system. I had never met them and had not been invited to do so. One thing in my favour was that Little Miss Beautiful was very bright and very independent so she was not going to be bullied by anybody.

I did not see her for a few days and then a few more until it was nearly a week. I began to worry. Had she got me out of her system? Why had she not been round? Had Adam killed her? I needed to find out.

Her father's factory was called Przybyszewski Sp.z o.o. (Ltd). So I went to the local chemist and asked if anybody spoke English. They all shook their heads.

"*Sprechen zie deutsch*?" one woman asked.

"*Ein bissien. Haben zie ein telephone directory bitter*?" I replied. To my utter astonishment they produced one immediately and in no time I had found the Przybyszewski Ltd. telephone number. The German speaking lady made the call and suddenly and totally unexpectedly I had Katarzyna's family addresses in my hand. It was that simple. Thank god I had learnt a little German while stationed there. I didn't think she would be at the main house so I plumped for the city apartment. Wichrowe Wzgorze (Wuthering Heights) 35/106 was the address.

One of the big advantages of living in my new flat was that outside there was a taxi rank. Every morning I took the same taxi to work and had become mates with Wiesiek, a crazy Pole with a beat-up old Mercedes. His German was worse than mine but, with all three languages at our disposal, we managed to communicate surprisingly well. He would often have a black eye as he was always getting into trouble with husbands. Wiesiek was just like my old friend Sniffy Snodgrass. He wanted to screw every girl he saw. For me, this was most odd, as he was very happily married to Yvonna, a typical Polish stunner, but he just could not keep his dick in his trousers. Somehow his wife put up with him.

I went straight from the chemist to the taxi rank and he was there. I gave him the address and off we went to Wuthering Heights via the nearest florist. The main entrance of Block 106 was open so I walked up the stairs and stood opposite number thirty five. I knocked on the door. The lady who opened the door must have been Katarzyna's mother as the look on her face was not a warm welcoming one. I thrust the bunch of roses towards her; she took them and smiled a little.

"Katarzyna, is she here?" I said, desperately trying to look over her shoulder.

She shook her head and started muttering about something which I couldn't really hear but it did not matter as I would not have understood anyway. She suddenly stopped, looked at me again, gave me a wry smile and ushered me in. Katarzyna was in bed with flu and had been for a week. As soon as she realised I was there, she jumped out of bed and in front of her mother and siblings gave me a huge hug.

Kasia, as all her family called her, had two sisters and two brothers. Luiza was twenty-one; Zbigniew seventeen, Ewa fifteen and little Oskar was three. Her mother was only five years older than me and her father seven. I was invited to sit down, given a piece of cake and a cup of tea and, after they had all finished staring at me as though I was some very rare zoo exhibit, I returned to my flat with my amazing girl.

The next morning Kasia woke feeling much better and so did I; apparently 'Mother' liked me. It was a drizzly Saturday morning and so we stayed in bed. I got up about noon and went to the local market to buy some lunch. Kasia had a bath. When I got back there was a little old lady in the corridor. She was jumping up and down, pointing at my front door and screaming, "*Pani! Pani! Pani!*"

When she saw me she stopped ranting and collapsed in a heap on the floor. My first concern was Kasia so I quickly opened the door to find her relaxing in the bath. I returned to the old bag. She must have been my neighbour as the adjacent door was ajar, so I picked her up, carried her in and put her on the sofa. She suddenly opened her eyes and screamed at me to get out.

Our plan for the evening was dinner at 'Tarots' followed by a spot of 'dancin 'n' romancin', but as we were leaving the flat my landlord, Mr Sarnowski, and his six foot five son arrived. He was a great landlord because he used to ring me in the office at least twice a week to make sure everything was okay and if anything broke he'd have it fixed immediately. So I was very surprised to see him and his son in the block at 8:30pm on a Saturday night. I knew there was something wrong when he and his son stopped and stood side by side in the corridor, preventing anyone from passing.

"Hello Mr. Sarnowski, anything wrong?" I asked.

"You must leave my premises immediately!" he shouted.

"Hang on a minute. What is going on?"

"You must leave now," he insisted.

"Look I have no idea what's eating you but we have a contract in which it clearly states that one month's notice must be given by either party on termination."

"Mr. Miller I thought you were a reasonable, well-behaved man, but you are clearly not. You have been bringing the reputation of this building down with your loud music, blaring television and drunken sex parties with all those girls."

I thought, *this is unreal*. I don't have a radio or a television and the only person to have ever visited was Kasia. Perhaps it was a previous tenant or someone else in the block? Anyway I explained all of this very clearly to him and he calmed down to the point when he agreed that I could stay.

A few days later I received a fax in the office from Mr. Sarnowski demanding again that I leave immediately. He was not prepared to discuss matters and if I was not out within twenty-four hours he would call the police and have me arrested. He further advised me that my disgusting behaviour had made any contract null and void and, according to his solicitor, he could kick me out now. I rang him immediately and demanded an explanation.

"There has been a committee meeting and the residents cannot put up with your constant sex parties any longer. They have advised me that if I do not get rid of you I will be forced to give up the flat."

"You know very well the only visitor I have is my girlfriend, Kasia. Are you telling me that I am not allowed visitors?"

"Well.....err.....well. Yes......visitors are allowed, but the committee..."

"Sod the committee. You're my landlord. Why don't you stand up for me?"

"You must leave now."

"Fuck you Sarnowski, you spineless shit!" And with that I slammed the phone down.

About three hundred yards from our block was a little bistro bar called 'The Bonin'. It was owned by a couple who lived in the block and run by their daughter, Magda and her husband. Magda spoke reasonable English and that evening, over a few beers, she explained what was going on.

The old bag, who was my neighbour and who had been shouting *Pani, Pani* which is Polish for girl/lady/woman, was mad. After the Second World War she had got herself pregnant by a British soldier in the hope he would do the decent thing and take her back to England but he dumped her instead. She gave birth to a girl, was rejected by her family and friends for her deviousness and had lived alone ever since. When her daughter found out years later she too vamoosed to look for her father. This dragon had been living in the block for as long as anyone could remember and had inveigled her way onto the committee. Seeing Kasia come and go made her convinced that the same fate would befall her so she started weaving a web of lies about me to avenge something that happened more than fifty years ago.

When we got back at midnight Sarnowski was waiting for us. While we were with Magda at the Bonin Bar, Mr. Sarnowski had been briefed by her father. This time he was deeply apologetic and said he had not realised about the old batty hen and of course we could stay. However, while all this had been going on Kasia had arranged for us to move in with her sister, Luiza in Sobieskiego, another large housing estate not far from Wuthering Heights. It was quite likely that, now the old bag's little ruse had been rumbled, she might try a more direct approach and shoot me, so we packed and left.

My parents knew my first marriage would never last and so before I went to Poland my father asked me that if I ever got serious about another girl would it be possible for them to meet her before anything happened. It wasn't a case of giving her their seal of approval; they said it would just be nice.

I was totally besotted with Kasia and since it was my mother's birthday soon, I thought at this point the time was ideal for popping over to the UK for a long weekend. I told the Serbs that I had to go back to the UK to finalise my divorce which was partially the case.

When we got back to Poznan Goran announced that we were going to open an office in Wroclaw, a city about two hours' drive south of Poznan. The Poznan operation had slowed down considerably, so we needed to find another source of income. Somehow, the nasty bitch that was Bojana, had found out about Kasia and so I was sent to help Goran get Wroclaw going and she stayed in Poznan. This was not in my plans but I had no choice. Kasia used to come down on the train with me and we stayed in this filthy bedsit with Goran and a couple of the translators. Business was a disaster as the whole operation had not been planned properly and Wroclaw haemorrhaged money. In the meantime Bojana was getting out of her depth trying to run Poznan on her own and started cutting corners.

One afternoon Goran just told me that he'd had enough and walked out. I rang Anton immediately and told him that I thought that Goran and Bojana were probably going to clean out the safety deposit boxes and do a runner.

Anton rang the Poznan office and spoke to Marta. He told her to nick the safety deposit box keys from Bojana's handbag which was always lying under her desk and give them to the hotel manager. He then rang the manager and asked him to give the keys to me when I returned. Finally he asked her to get Bojana to ring him ASAP. While all this was going on I had to explain to all the workers in Wroclaw what had happened. I also had to tell them that there was no money to pay them as Goran had buggered off back to Poznan with what was left.

Thank god Kasia was with me otherwise I would have been lynched on the spot. We only had enough money for our fare back to Poznan and after I closed the office, we caught a late train. When we arrived, I took Kasia back to Luiza's flat by taxi and then went to Hotel Poznan. There was no sign of Goran or Bojana, so I got the keys and the boxes from the hotel manager and opened up the office, closing and locking the door behind me.

There was about one hundred and twenty million zloty in the boxes. I changed all but about fifteen million zloty into US dollars in the hotel and then rang Anton at his home. The '*Terrible Two*' had been sacked and told that if they knew what was good for them then they'd leave Poland immediately as Rupert's new girlfriend's elder brothers were Mafia connected and very angry indeed.

"Rupert, close down the office, look after the computer, stationary and money. You have a good Christmas and give me a call in the New Year. I am working on a new venture for you."

With all that cash bulging out of my pockets I scurried back to the flat and broke the news.

"Where might you be sent after Christmas?" Kasia asked nervously.

"I have no idea but wherever it is will you come with me?"

"Yes, please!"

We had quick baths and then made wild passionate love until we were both covered in sweat. I then lay on top of her and said.

"Will you marry me?"

"I'll think about it."

"Well is that a yes or a no?"

"I'll tell you tomorrow evening." And with that Kasia rolled over and went fast to sleep. I tossed and turned in turmoil for hours but sleep finally got the better of me. The next morning when I woke I repeated the question.

"Look, I'll tell you my decision this evening. I am going out for the day and I'll see you at my mother's flat at seven this evening okay?" With that Kasia got up, showered, dressed and left. I moped about the flat in the morning, went to the Green Pub for a Guinness or two and then had a Chinese. After lunch I went back to the flat for some much needed sleep.

I woke at six which gave me just enough time to 'shit, shower and shave', before heading off to Wuthering Heights for my exam results. I got to their flat at precisely 7:00pm and on this occasion the door to the main block was closed so I had to press the buzzer. The door was opened immediately and I looked up the stairs and saw Kasia standing outside the flat with a very silly smile on her face.

"Yes or no?" I called out to her.

"YES! YES! YES!" Kasia replied while running down the stairs and jumped into my arms. We kissed madly and after about ten minutes Kasia's mother came down and almost had to chuck a bucket of water over us. Much merrymaking ensued and later that evening Kasia told me that she hadn't gone to ask her family's approval and permission earlier in the day, she had gone to tell them that she was going to marry me. She had expected a fierce battle but, much to her surprise, there was no resistance at all. The next day, after I had stopped pinching myself, I went into the centre of Poznan to buy an engagement ring. I found a very nice pretty gold ring with a green emerald in a pawn shop.

The following day was Christmas Eve 1993 and I was invited to join the family for a traditional Christmas Eve dinner. In Poland, the large Christmas celebrations are done on Christmas Eve and the traditional food they eat is carp. Such is the demand for carp, that even one of the old Olympic swimming pools in Poznan has been converted into a carp farm. The idea is to buy the carp live, stick the fish in the bath, bless it on Christmas Eve, boil them or fry them and then devour them. This disgusting fish is served with some type of brown gravy that does not improve the flavour, but Kasia and her entire family couldn't stuff enough of this sodden cardboard down their gullets.

If you take a spoon of Mississippi river mud and mix it with old fish guts then you have the texture of carp and, more than likely, the taste. I have never met anyone, apart from a Pole, who disagrees with me on this subject. The smell is pretty nasty too. Incidentally, carp is an anagram of crap.

I was not due to call Anton for another week and I still had all the business's cash on me. Anton had told me to pay myself out of this money but not how much.

I had a very old friend who half owned a farm house near a place called Decin, just over the border in the Czech Republic. I suggest to Kasia that maybe we could go and see him for New Year. She thought this was a wonderful idea and so I rang Marian Svjeda and a few days later we caught the sleeper train to Prague. Fortunately we had a compartment all to ourselves but the beds were about as wide as a slat from a Venetian blind and just as comfortable. There was no point in getting undressed as we knew that the train guards, border guards, ticket collectors and an assortment of other officials would be disturbing us throughout the entire journey.

At the border Adolf and his team barged into our compartment.

"Passports!" They screamed. We handed them over and they flicked through them in the most unpleasant and aggressive way. They then pulled out the stamping machine and seemed to stamp every other page before handing them back.

"Do you have any money on you?" This question threw me slightly. I had about six thousand korunas on me so I told them.

"You are only allowed to bring two hundred into the country. Don't you have any dollars?"

"No."

"If you cannot pay your fine in dollars you must leave the train now and I must confiscate your korunas." I was about to explode. What fucking fine? Kasia quickly pulled me back and took over the negotiations as she knew damn well I'd screw it up. She pouted her lips, smiled, wiggled her bottom and played the poor little lost girl to perfection. He, of course, melted, apologised and left the compartment. We managed to grab a little sleep and at dawn we arrived in Prague. Our train to Decin was not for another six hours so we strolled around the city.

The farmhouse we were going to spend New Year in was jointly owned by Sjveda and James Hardy. James was the son of some very old friends of my parents. Sjveda was a documentary filmmaker who was always in trouble with the authorities. They thought he was a British spy. Sjveda had met James in London in the early seventies on one of his documentary 'fact finding' missions and together they had decided to buy the farm house, known as Hardy's Castle.

In 1976 Hardy and Sjveda invited my parents, me and Julian to spend Christmas and New Year with them at Hardy's Castle. The plan was to drive there in my father's green Rolls-Royce. When we got to Czechoslovakia all hell broke loose. The Border guards took one look at the Rolls-Royce and decided they were going to go through it with a fine-toothed comb. They had all the suitcases out in the snow and some grease monkey thoroughly checked the engine. They did not find anything until they opened Julian's suitcase. In it they found a novel he was reading about the Second World War. I cannot remember the name of the book but the front cover depicted a swastika covered in blood. This got them very excited and they tried to arrest him for attempting to bring in subversive propaganda into their country. Julian was fourteen, a severe haemophiliac and quite obviously a spy. My mother flew into a rage and started hitting the guards with a rolled up *Financial Times*. This was going to do one of two things: either we would all be shot on the spot or they would be so shocked and perplexed they would let us go. Fortunately the latter prevailed and very shortly we were on our way to Prague.

We were booked into Hotel Intercontinental and arrived at about 8.00pm on Christmas Eve. Our rooms were very basic and mother spent the next hour checking all of the rooms for KGB bugs. There were no loos in the rooms so you had to use the unisex ablutions at the end of the corridor. All the toilets were smashed so when you had a pee it ended up all over your shoes.

During this trip, Svjeda's parents had invited us for dinner but when we finally got back to our hotel at about one in the morning there was no one around to give us our keys. I leaned over the reception desk to see if I could find our keys and to my surprise the receptionist was lying on the floor with an empty bottle of vodka beside her. The bell boy had passed out half-way up the stairs and we found the night manager and another receptionist, pissed as rats, having it off on a kitchen table. Prague really had changed. The hotel I had stayed in seventeen years ago was now a five-star luxury Hilton.

The train line from Prague to Decin ran alongside the River Elbe and the views of the mountains dotted with castles were quite magnificent. As there were no seats available in any of the compartments we camped in the dining car where we had a good, but very expensive late lunch.

Sjveda met us and took us to Hardy's Castle where we met his wife, three small children and numerous friends. The farmhouse was large, made entirely out of wood and each room had its own stove. There was no central heating and, as it was minus seventeen degrees outside, it was imperative that you kept your own stove fully stoked. There was plenty of coal and wood, and all we did for five days was eat and drink. Kasia never really drank but on the first night she got so drunk she fell off her chair and I had to carry her to bed. She repeated this feat on the second night and Svjeda leant over to me and asked.

"Rupert, are you really intending to marry that girl?"

"Oh yes, absolutely." I replied.

When we got back to Poznan I bought some telephone tokens, found a phone that had not been trashed and rang Anton.

"Rupert, you are going to Vilnius in Lithuania. Buy yourself a plane ticket; take the computer, stationary and the money with you. A chap called 'Larry' will meet you at the airport."

Chapter Seven

I broke the news to Kasia when she got back from her usual 'gossip with Mother'.

"Can I come too?" She beamed.

"Do you really want to go to Lithuania? I mean, I don't even know where it is; do you?"

"Of course I do silly, it is next to Poland and if you are going then I'm coming with you. When do you have to go?"

"As soon as I have bought the tickets."

On our way to the Travel Agent in the centre of Poznan we stopped off at Wuthering Heights to break the news to her family. This was too much for her mother who thought I was totally mad to go and try and sell timeshare in probably one of the most dangerous cities in Eastern Europe. Me going was one thing, but her beloved Kasia was out of the question. After much family consultation it was agreed that I'd go and check it out and, if everything worked to plan, then Kasia would follow.

There were no direct flights from Poznan to Vilnius so I'd have to take a train to Warsaw. The next flight to Vilnius was in two days' time at eight in the morning. My plan was for both of us to go to Warsaw and stay at the Marriot hotel. I could have taken the night train from Poznan to Warsaw on the eve of the flight but, as we had all this company money, I thought a little spoiling in the Marriot would be rather nice. Kasia and her brother helped me pack all the stuff I had to take with me, including the computer and he drove us to the station where we caught the afternoon train to Warsaw. I was very excited and also a little apprehensive. After all, I was about to leave the woman I had just found, disappear to a country full of cut-throats and start a business with people I had never met.

The Marriot was the best hotel in Warsaw and we had a large room near the top floor overlooking the entire snow-covered city. We had a huge king size bed and Kasia fell in love with the bathroom. I booked an early morning call for 5:30am and then we went down to the bar, had a few drinks and then onto dinner in one of the hotel restaurants.

The next morning I woke up and looked at my watch. It was 8:00am and my plane was no doubt trundling down the runway on its way to Vilnius. I woke Kasia and asked her if she had heard the alarm call. She hadn't and rolled over back to sleep. I picked up the phone and rang reception.

"Hello, this is Rupert Miller, why did I not get my early morning call? I've now missed my flight."

"You did not order one Sir."

"Oh yes I did. I saw the receptionist clearly mark it down on my check-in card."

"Right, Sir. I'll look into it."

"Thank you."

About ten minutes later the phone rang.

"Mr. Miller? This is the front desk manager. I am terribly sorry, you were absolutely right. I cannot apologise enough for our mistake but I'll have to discuss it with the General Manager when he comes in at nine."

Shortly after nine there was a knock at the door. It was the General Manager.

He accepted full responsibility and told me that he would get me on the next flight to Vilnius and in the meantime the hotel, its restaurants and bars were at our disposal completely free of charge. This terrific news became even better when I found out that the next flight to Vilnius was not u[illegible] the next day. We had another twenty-four hours at [illegible]

I immediately ordered room service. We [illegible] English breakfast and then Kasia went and got ful[illegible] at the hotel beauty salon. As it was snowing heavily we decided not to venture out. Anyway, by the time Kasia had finished at the salon, it was time for pre-lunch cocktails. Lobster Mornay, followed by Isles Flotant and washed down with a very good bottle of Chablis were a great primer for sex. A good sleep ensued which prepared us for dinner. Kasia had an enormous Caesar Salad and I opted for a simple fillet steak au poivre and a nice bottle of Burgundy. After dinner we went to the downstairs bar for coffee, chocolates and cognac. No such mistakes were made the following morning as, not only did they ring our room too early, they also sent up a bell boy to knock on the door. To further ensure we left on time they took all my clobber down to a waiting taxi which they also paid for.

It was soon time to depart and, as I hate protracted farewells, I gave my darling Kasia a huge hug, kissed her and then went straight through passport control into the departure lounge.

There were only ten of us on the bus that took us across the ice packed runway towards the plane and I had visions of it sliding off the runway and crashing. These thoughts became very vivid when I caught sight of the plane that we were about to get on; Lithuanian Airlines Flight TE142 was a very old plane indeed. It was no doubt some Russian make built at the same time as the Ark. It had two jet engines that seemed to be held on with binding twine and was absolutely filthy. I thought, *I have got to get off this bus and go straight back to Poznan. I really do not want to die in a plane crash having collided with some Eastern European mountain.* However it was now too late to go back as we had arrived at the plane. We were ushered up the steps and told that we could sit where we liked. I made a beeline for a seat at the ack as this would mean I would be the last one to hit the mountain. I sat down and started looking at the various bits of airline junk that you normally find in the pocket in front of you. Just like the magazines at the doctor's surgery at home, the Lithuanian Airlines version of *Knitting Weekly* was dated pre 1968. In addition to the in-flight magazine, I also found a sick bag, a torn safety instruction card and some empty sweet wrappers from the previous flight. Everything on board was pea green; even the stewardesses were dressed in green. The windows had not been spray-painted; they had been very badly painted with a cheap brush as many of the bristles were stuck in the paint.

On British Airways flights there was always a much practiced safety show. Two or three, depending upon the size of the plane, plumpish stewardesses with smiles like synchronised swimmers waved their arms about, pointed at the exits and demonstrated how to use your life jacket. In contrast, the Lithuanian stewardesses had a far more practical approach. Read the safety card if you can be bothered. The Lithuanian Airlines motto was, no doubt; '*If* we crash, we die'. Judging by everything I had witnessed so far the motto should read. '*When* we crash we die'.

So Lithuanian Airline Flight TE142 took off, and as we did, all the backs of the seats that were unoccupied fell forward. After we'd taken off they all fell back again. The flight was only one hour and much to my surprise the brunch we were given was very good. As we approached our destination I could see Vilnius and by Christ it looked bleak and very cold. Coming into land I saw about thirty old Russian biplanes with their winter coats on and thought that I was about to go back in time to the Dark Ages.

Lithuanian Airline pilots do not land smoothly. They like to drop the aircraft onto the tarmac but I was later told that they always do this in icy and snowy conditions to minimise the chances of skidding. We came to a halt, got off the plane and onto a bus. Fuck it was cold. I had never been so cold in my life. The ice on the bus windows was thicker on the inside. The bus drove fifty feet to the terminal building and slid to a halt, narrowly missing our baggage trolley.

Vilnius airport was weird. The departure lounge was brand new and looked like a space station. The arrivals lounge looked like Poznan railway station and was just as scary. After we passed through customs all the luggage from Flight TE142 was dumped in a heap in the corner. I quickly retrieved the computer and my five pieces of luggage which I then sat on while waiting for Larry to pick me up. After about half an hour there was still no sign of Larry and I was beginning to attract the attention of a bunch of very dangerous looking taxi drivers. There was one who kept staring at me. He was quite short but had an evil face, shaved head, a few black teeth and a scar cut from his right ear lobe to the corner of his mouth. A few more minutes passed and he came up to me,"You want taxi?"

"No thank you. I am waiting for someone."

"Your friend is late, isn't he?" he whispered." You'll need one of us sooner or later." He smirked at me and walked back to his taxi. Larry had obviously not got my fax or he had been delayed or even murdered.

Over the next thirty minutes other taxi drivers tried their luck but I was buggered if I was going to get into any of their taxis. I was sure Larry would turn up eventually. As none of his colleagues had been successful in luring me into a cab, one driver came over and without asking, picked up my luggage and started trying to put it in his taxi. I jumped up and stopped him. He became quite aggressive.

"You give me twenty dollars. I take you to town and no trouble." This was an order not a suggestion. At that moment a large well-dressed man approached us and started shouting at the taxi driver in what must have been Lithuanian. When he had finished the driver got into his cab and drove off.

"You look as though you need some assistance." He was an American. I explained my position.

"Look you better come with me, I have a car outside. Where are you going?"

"Hotel Lietuva please."

He was a regular visitor to Lithuania and managed to arrange for me to leave most of my luggage in the airport office until I could pick it up the next day. The American dropped me off at the hotel and wished me lots of luck in whatever I was doing there.

Finding Larry or what was left of him was my main priority so I went up to the reception.

Excuse me please. Do you have a Mr. Larry Bedford staying here?" The Receptionist completely ignored me. She wasn't busy; in fact she was reading a magazine that had, as far as I could see, nothing to do with the running of a hotel. I tried again.

"Hello. Do you speak English?"

This time she looked up at me, picked up the phone and dialed an internal number. In a few minutes another girl appeared and asked me if she could help.

"Yes please. I am trying to find out if a Mr. Larry Bedford is staying in the hotel." She looked at the computer, checked a few pieces of paper that were lying on the desk and said, "No. We do not."

No wonder Larry had not met me. I bet he wasn't even in the country and it was definitely the correct hotel, no mistake there. I now needed time to plan my next course of action. My first instinct was to fly straight back to Poland, keep all the money and get a job there, but I decided not to be too hasty and found a small bar in the corner of the hotel. I ordered a beer and just watched people walk in and out of the hotel. It soon became apparent that this was not like having afternoon tea at the Ritz. The hotel foyer was crawling with big guys carrying mobile phones that looked like bricks, wearing ankle length leather jackets and sporting very short haircuts. A few of them were accompanied by dolly birds with thick fur coats and Gucci handbags. *That's it*, I thought, *I'm going back to my girl now*.

I finished my beer and was about to get up when I saw, what could only be described as an Englishman, walking towards my table. He was virtually bald, had a stupid grin on his face and a huge beer belly that he was kicking along the floor in front of him. He stopped, picked up his belly, stuffed it back in his trousers and said.

"Hello, I'm Larry. You must be Rupert. Have you brought all of the stuff and the money?"

"Yes, and thanks for meeting me at the airport!" I joked but it went straight over his head. He was registered at the hotel but had checked in as Lawrence Bedford. Half of me was relieved to see a friendly face but the other half was rather pissed off as now I'd have to stay. Anyway we swapped pleasantries and then to my utter amazement Woody Allen walked into the hotel, spotted us and came over to our table.

"I've put an ad in the paper, Larry," he said and then sat down. This was John Holmes, an American Woody Allen clone. The three of us were going to start selling Anton's Spanish timeshare apartments in Vilnius.

It was too late to really do anything that afternoon so I checked into the hotel and went back to the airport to collect the luggage I had left behind. The hotel provided a car and a driver named Romasc. He spoke a little English and was about six foot ten so I was not worried about going back to the airport in the slightest. Romasc was a big Manchester United Fan and had Bobby Charlton and George Best stickers all over his car. He could not stop talking about Manchester United Football Club, and when I told him I was born in Manchester and worked in Manchester, he almost crashed the car. We finally got back to the hotel at 7:00pm and Romasc helped me carry everything to my room. I thanked him and he gave me an almost fatal bear hug.

"You Manchester Man. You my good new friend." He then left but I now felt that I had at least one ally in Lithuania.

Hotel Lietuva was a state run disaster. It had twenty two floors, had taken ten years to build and was losing fifteen million dollars a year. The reason why we had chosen it was that it had two conference halls which we intended to use for the timeshare presentations. There was a standard hotel restaurant, very similar to the one in Hotel Poznan, three bars and the Panorama Club on the twenty-second floor.

The pricing structure in the bars was bizarre. At the front of the hotel the small bar charged four litas (Lithuanian currency) for a coffee and the bar in the centre of the hotel only charged one lita, but it was the same coffee. The other bar, The Black Bar, did not serve coffee. The whole interior of the hotel was pine and had the warmth of a doctor's waiting room. The bedrooms were pokey and far too hot as you could not open the windows and all central heating was state controlled.

The advertisement John had put in the newspaper was for staff. We needed translators, office staff, sales reps and receptionists to help us run our business. Larry was the boss as he had bought the franchise from Anton. John and I were on an equal footing but he made it perfectly clear to me that, as he was older and had been in the business far longer than me, then he felt that he was second in command. This was fine by me so I let Woody strut about like a peacock.

The advert had invited anyone interested to come to Hotel Lietuva for an interview at 10:00am so after our breakfast we went to the conference hall and waited. In the first hour more than five hundred people turned up looking for jobs. The hotel management was furious as at least two hundred of them were pretty close to being vagrants and the hotel did not have nearly enough security staff to control them. Later that day they told us that all the hotel toilet rolls had been stolen and the state of some of the cubicles beggared belief.

The first thing we had to do was to find the best English speakers so we could communicate with the others. Next, we needed a pool of about thirty sales reps, so we selected the best dressed and best looking. Finally, we needed to fill the office staff roles. A pool of sales reps is needed as they are notoriously unreliable. After a few hours of interviewing, we had our team. Out of the five hundred applicants, we chose only thirty-eight. Some of the men we turned away became very abusive, and had it not been for Romasc and the security guards, they may have offered us some violence. Many of the girls were in floods of tears and were on their knees begging us for a job. It made us wonder just how bad unemployment was in Lithuania in 1994.

Larry and John spent the rest of the day training them all and I was sent shopping with one of the translators to get various things for the office. This did not take long so I spent the rest of the afternoon wandering around Vilnius.

Vilnius, the capital of Lithuania, is the geographical centre of Europe and in 1994 had a population of 600,000 out of Lithuania's total of 3.7 million. The city itself dated back to the fourteenth century and was built on the River Neris, which boasted large floating ice packs from December to March. I was soon to learn that the temperature could drop to minus thirty below for weeks on end and that is why the central heating was run by the state. At the end of October it would be switched on and on the fifteenth of April, it would be switched off. No argument. There were no thermostats to control the heating so you would find yourself freezing outside one minute and then roasting inside the next.

Like Poznan, the old town of Vilnius was absolutely charming. It reminded me of a little Cotswold village. Sadly most of the buildings were in a terrible state of repair and the attempts they seemed to be making to restore the place were wholly inadequate. For a start the scaffolding was wooden and always being stolen for firewood so folk could keep warm after the fifteenth of April each year. Mindless vandalism had damaged many buildings beyond repair, so they were just knocked down. There were a few pretty churches but the rest of Vilnius was like Poznan, a network of concrete high-rise housing estates.

After my informative stroll round the town I went back to the hotel. Larry and John had finished the training for the day and were sitting in the 'One Lit.' bar having a beer. They had arrived in Vilnius a few days before, both from selling timeshare in Portugal for Anton so they knew my connection. The money I had was to be used to pay for the start-up costs, and although seven thousand dollars seems very little, it bought a hell of a lot in Vilnius in 1994. Larry had found an office on the fourth floor of the Vilnius Architect Centre which was on the other side of the river to the hotel.

Our new office comprised of one large room and a slightly smaller one. The best part was the spectacular view of the ice floating down the Neris. Our flat packed furniture arrived as did our new office staff. The office manager was Rima. She was a Lithuanian school teacher and her English was better than mine. Working for the state education system paid virtually nothing so she joined us, even though she had a small family and understood that if we made no sales then nobody got paid. Giedrus was our gofer; Jurate; the receptionist; and Iewa, Maria and Mindaugas the main translators and canvassers.

By lunch time the telephone lines had been connected and the office furniture constructed. It was beginning to look like a business. We needed to put a door in the entrance to the smaller of the two rooms as this was going to be *our* office and a collections room, so privacy was essential. We asked the janitor if he could send up someone to install a door that we had bought. Not long after, Laurel and Hardy arrived, wearing dark blue overalls. Neither of them had any teeth, were well into their sixties and while they were fitting the door and the locks, spent the entire time arguing. At some point, one of them threatened the other with a claw hammer so Mindaugas had to intervene. It took them hours to complete this simple task but they did and the door closed properly and the locks worked. Their bill was 25 litas (£4) and two bottles of vodka. Gold Crown Resorts was born, prospects were invited to the presentations and we started selling timeshare.

Although business started quite well Larry said that it was essential that we found our own apartments as soon as possible as Anton was not going to pay for accommodation. After three days I found a lovely apartment in M.K.Ciurlionio Street, about one mile from the office. It was a very old fashioned flat and had a vast classic chandelier suspended from the ceiling. The apartment was the ground floor of a huge house and the entrance was in a courtyard and opened straight into the kitchen. Next to the kitchen was a tiny bathroom and opposite that was the door to the main house. Then there was the sitting room/bedroom which had an enormous raised fireplace in the corner. The fireplace was surrounded by white tiles and looked just like a vast chest of drawers with carved figures decorating the top. It was fully functional and provided much needed warmth as the heating system in the whole building was unreliable.

I had found this wonderful place thanks to Romasc, the Man United besotted hotel driver and so I went with him and Iewa to agree terms with the landlady. She had a mouth full of gold and looked just like a scarecrow. The flat belonged to her son who was on business in Russia for a few years. She told Iewa that she liked me and that I could have the place for US$ 300 per month on the grounds that I gave her a US$ 300 deposit immediately and that I would not invite females around. Remembering the problems I had in Lazurowa with Mr. Sarnowski I asked.

"Would it be alright if my wife came to live with me?"

"Oh, you have a wife. That's marvelous, of course. When is she arriving?" I had lied. Well, we were engaged, and that made me even more determined to get my Kasia over to Vilnius. I signed a six month contract, went back to the hotel and sent a telegram to Kasia to come as soon as possible. The next day I had a reply giving me full details of her arrival.

I was beginning to make some money, had a lovely flat but no wood. I made several enquiries about how to get wood but no one seemed to know. Romasc used to bring me the occasional log he had stolen from the forest, which I paid him for but this supply was soon exhausted and it was too much to expect him to keep nicking the stuff. I needed to find another legitimate source quickly.

By now it was nearly the end of January and getting colder day by day. The Neris had frozen over completely and there were piles of snow everywhere. Kasia was due to arrive the following week and I needed to make sure our nest was warm. I was woken early the next morning, which happened to be a Saturday, by the sound of banging coming from an apartment on the other side of the courtyard so I got up and investigated. To my delight there were a bunch of builders ripping out the old wooden flooring from a downstairs flat and putting them in a skip. I asked the foreman how much he wanted for them. He had so much rubble to remove that he offered to carry all the floorboards into my flat and I could have them for nothing. This was going to save him a packet on skip hire and I had enough wood for the winter.

These floorboards were all about eight to ten feet long and I did not have a saw to cut them up so they would fit on the fire. No problem I'll just go and buy one. I went to the hotel and asked for Romasc as he'd know where I could get a saw. Unfortunately it was his day off so I went to the taxi rank and jumped in the first Volga.

"Where to?" I assumed he asked.

"Shops... Err... Market.... Centrum? Please." I replied. He seemed to understand and we set off in roughly the right direction. Halfway into town there were some trees on the side of the road so I asked him to stop. I got out of the taxi, went over to one of the trees and with my arm shaped like a saw, pretended to saw the tree down. He looked at me sympathetically and was genuinely trying to understand the purpose of my mini charade. All of a sudden he got out of the taxi, opened the passenger door and beckoned me to get in. He knew exactly what I wanted and in no time at all we were at a rather shabby looking garden centre in the outskirts of Vilnius. They were selling trees, Christmas trees and nothing else. It was, after all, the end of January.

I had been remarkably stupid. Why hadn't I simply drawn a picture of a saw in the first place? It would have saved so much time and money. What a fool. Once he saw my 'saw' he drove me straight round to a hardware store only a few hundred yards from my flat where I bought a brand new stainless steel saw and a little hand axe and spent the rest of the day converting the floor boards into kindling and eighteen inch logs. Tomorrow was Sunday and the day Kasia was due to arrive, so I went to bed early but could not sleep.

Her flight was due at 2:00pm but terrible snowstorms all over Eastern Europe delayed everything. I finally got to the airport with Romasc just before the scheduled arrival time. It had taken us an hour and a half but it did not matter as Kasia's plane had not even left Warsaw. I waited and waited and her flight finally arrived, five hours late. Thankfully Romasc stayed too and he dropped us of at the flat which we only just managed to get into. A mountain of snow had drifted up against the door and all the cars in the courtyard were completely buried. I lit a fire, introduced her to the scarecrow, cooked some supper and then we made love in front of the fire for hours. My life was back to normal.

After a promising start, business began, for no discernible reason, to tail off so we had to double our efforts just to survive. Larry and John ran the afternoon presentations, but I had to be in the office all day in case anyone who had paid a deposit came in and either paid the balance or tried to cancel. If they tried to cancel it would be a question of a total re-sale, which could take hours. After a full day in the office I'd join them for the evening event. Another problem was with the Lithuanian work ethic; it didn't seem as sharp as what I was used to in Poland. I assumed this had to go with being geographically closer to the Soviet Union. There a job was a job for life and there seemed to be no incentive to show initiative as it did not result in any monetary reward. Keep your nose clean, clock in, clock off and collect the paltry peanuts at the end of the month and you'd be spared possible interrogation by the KGB. Also many Lithuanian businesses were closed on Mondays. Our theory was that they would get so drunk over the weekend that they needed Mondays to recover.

This made doing business difficult. It was impossible to get a straight answer or to get them to do anything on their own. Iewa, one of the translators and the girl who helped me deal with collections and cancellations, appeared to be very switched on. She had a good university degree. Her job was pretty much the same every day, but every morning she'd arrive at work and ask me what she had to do. If I, Larry or John were not there for some reason, she'd do nothing. Maybe the system she had been brought up in had made her shit scared of making a mistake? Their total lack of energy, drive, ambition or willingness to help drove us totally potty. We wanted to reward them for hard and good work. They seemed to want to be beaten with a stick like a mule. Not our style.

Early on in our venture I needed some more pencils so I could fill out the accounts ledger.

"Where can I buy some pencils?" A simple question.

"Pencils?... Cor… Gosh… Err… I've no idea." A standard reply.

"Look, you live here. One of you must know where I can find a stationery shop?" They would just stand there, looking up at the ceiling for divine inspiration or seeing if the floor had the answer. It was mind-boggling. All I wanted to do was to buy a simple pencil, but they did not want to help. Their stock reply was always the same.

"You must understand, we're Lithuanians and you are in our country." When in Rome… Dozens would turn up at the office looking for employment but most of them did not want to work. We found one guy who we thought was excellent. He spoke English, was well presented and very keen. We thought he'd make a good sales rep and a part-time translator, so we offered him a job. He was over the moon. The next morning he did not turn up and we could not get hold of him as he, like most of the others, was not on the phone.

However, the following morning he did and brought his brother with him. He told us that he would only work for us if we employed his brother too and that if this was not possible he would tell the local newspapers that we were a bunch of con artists only interested in stealing from poor Lithuanians.

Geidrus, our large gofer, suddenly saw his job going up in smoke, along with everybody else's, so he marched over to this guy, picked him up by the throat, pinned him to the wall and started muttering to him. This guy's brother probably wasn't his brother after all as he scarpered as fast as he could. Giedrus then let him go and he too made a hasty exit. I asked Rima what he had said.

"If I read one bad story in any newspaper about Gold Crown Resorts I will break your fucking neck." Well it must have worked as we did not get the promised bad press or any other similar threats.

The most staggering thing about the Lithuanians was their telephone technique or lack of it. All our conversations with customers had to be done via a translator, so I would ask them to pick up the phone and dial the number. It would ring twice and then they would put the phone down.

"They are not in."

"What do you mean, they are not in? You did not give them a chance to answer. Please try them again and hold on much longer, okay?" Obviously telephonophobia was pandemic in Lithuania. Answering the phone caused even more problems as they would: carry on nattering for ages; never write anything down; and when they had finished, they'd have no idea who was on the other end or what the conversation was about. It really was as bad as that. It happened all the time and the excuse was always, "I'm a Lithuanian….etc.etc."

Kasia was with me so I was very happy. She used to come to the office and was able to communicate with everyone because, like Poles, the staff spoke Russian. Sometimes she would go to the museums and art galleries and we found a very progressive art shop where we bought an easel, some paints and several canvases so she could practice her painting, an activity she adored. Kasia was up for this adventure.

Larry, on the other hand, had a comfort seeking Hungarian girlfriend who came over but hated Vilnius and gave Larry an ultimatum. As business was not great, Larry quit and John took over the franchise. The next week we made no sales and the wheels started to fall off the whole business. We were down to our last few hundred dollars and in serious danger of having to flee the country.

John and I sat down one evening after another disastrous presentation to plan what we were going to do. Our first problem was the conference hall we were using. It was vast and unfriendly, so we decided to move to a much smaller one next to the Black Bar. We decided to give a single rose to each wife who came to a presentation, offer them champagne instead of coffee and increase the prices. The idea was to present the timeshare properties as a luxury product that only a few could afford and were available on a strictly first-come first-served basis. We had just enough money for two more presentations, but we would do them in style.

Miraculously it worked. In the next two presentations we took over US$ 35,000 and we were back in business. Confidence grew, which led to more and more sales and cancellations never happened. Some excellent press really helped and we actually had to turn people away. We had found the right formula and had a steady stream of rich Lithuanians eager to give us their money. This new breed of customer paid in dollars, the ones they wanted to launder, and buying timeshare property in Spain gave them the perfect vehicle. We started to make good money. John concentrated on the presentations, I looked after the accounts and we both did the sales.

We appointed our best Lithuanian sales rep, Aida, as sales manager which was a brilliant move for two reasons. Firstly, she had become good friends with Kasia so I got to know what they were all thinking and secondly, although only twenty-two, she marshalled her troops extremely well. She introduced a sales league table which I supported with a bonus system. To our surprise this made the reps ultra-competitive and we now had a smoothly run, money-making machine. However, what we had not anticipated, was the effect that this new found wealth would have on them.

In 1994 the average monthly wage in Lithuania was only US$40 or 160 litas. Our office staff would frequently take home 1500 litas a month and our top sales reps between 3000 & 4000 litas a month, twenty-five times the national average monthly take home pay. For them it was like winning the Lottery every month.

Apart from Giedrus, Mindaugas and a couple of sales reps, who were all single, the rest of our staff were young married women with small children. The typical Lithuanian male was a bit like the African lion. He slept all day, sent the wife out to catch the zebra and then ate the fillet himself leaving the scraps for her and the kids.

Well our female employees suddenly forgot about zebras and started going out for lunch and pampered themselves with the latest outfits and cosmetics. They bought new furniture for the house, clothes for the kids and suddenly realised that the capitalist system was far better than the old communist one. They had money in their purses and lots of it. Their lackadaisical husbands could not stomach the idea that their weak and feeble wives were now the bread winners. We lost quite a few sales reps because their husbands preferred to live in abject poverty rather than swallow their pride and let their wives drag the family out of the gutter. Sometimes we could not let the reps work as they would turn up for the presentations with black eyes and bruised arms.

To counter this, we tried to employ more male reps but they were invariably late, no good, drunk or told us that we were doing everything wrong and, for a fee, would tell us how to improve things. One day we lost Iewa. She translated, dealt with the clients in the office, helped with the accounts and became the pay clerk – obviously a very important member of the team. One day her husband came to the office. He was very drunk, very angry and armed with a bread knife. His mission was to kill me and started screaming at me, accusing me of screwing his wife and corrupting her. He lunged at me with the knife but he was so drunk the alcohol rendered his attack useless and he tumbled to the ground, the knife falling out of harm's way. Giedrus came to the rescue once again and pinned him to the floor. Rima wanted to call the police but Iewa said she'd take him home once he'd sobered up. They sat him in a chair and poured black coffee down his throat for three hours. Rima spent all her energy trying to explain to him that Gold Crown Resorts was the best thing that had ever happened to him and Iewa and he should embrace his wife's good fortune not destroy it. The next day Iewa came to work as normal but promptly resigned. I pleaded with her to stay, but she quite rightly pointed out that, if she did, she would just get more beatings and our business would suffer. I noticed that she had fresh bruises and I never saw or heard of her ever again.

The other big problem was a psychological one. We have all heard of the horror stories of some lottery winners. Suddenly a normal family wins several million and a couple of years later you read in the tabloids that they are now divorced, had affairs, entered into disastrous business ventures, lost it all and owe some loan shark a stack of money.

We employed one nineteen year old called Raimonda. She was very pretty and a terrific sales rep. On her first night she made two sales and earned herself over US$150. After the presentation she came up to me and asked me for an advance saying she was skint. I had been in the same predicament myself on many occasions so I gave her 150 litas as it was Friday.

On Monday morning she came into the office and all she was wearing was an old jumper, no bra, a pair of hold up stockings and some old army boots with no laces. Her make-up was smeared all over her face and she was in floods of tears. She demanded to see me so Mindaugas, Iewa's replacement, took her into my office, sat her down and tried to translate. She was completely hysterical and would not remain seated. She pranced round the office like a caged panther, waving her arms about and sobbing uncontrollably. Her sobbing suddenly turned to crazy laughter and then, just as quickly, back to sobbing. After about twenty minutes Mindaugas managed to calm her down and she sat on the chair in front of me.

"Raimonda, please tell us, what is the matter?" I asked.

"I need some money!" she screamed.

"But Raimonda, I gave you some on Friday, have you spent it?"

"It's my fucking money; I can do what I fucking like with it you fucking bastard!"

"Look Raimonda, it's payday soon and I broke all the company rules giving you that advance on Friday but if you are really desperate, as you obviously are, then I will give you half of the balance due to you now and the rest on payday, okay?" She stopped sobbing and broke out into a broad smile.

"Thank you Mr. Rupert, thank you very much. You are very kind."

Payday came and went and there was no sign of Raimonda. We got in touch with her landlady who told us that Raimonda had been taken into hospital. With the money I had given her she had bought pretty dresses and lots of perfume and cosmetics and had spent all her time dressing and undressing in front of the mirror. She used to lie on her bed naked, cover herself in money and shout, "I'm rich, I'm rich," and then burst into floods of tears. She finally lost total control and, according to the doctors, had gone stark raving mad. A few weeks later we learned that Raimonda had committed suicide on her twentieth birthday.

Chapter Eight

Counterfeiting has been around probably since currency was invented. A recent example is the skill of the forgers in North Korea, where from the 1970s onward, they have been perfecting US dollars to fund operations against South Korea. These craftsman have become so good at copying the US$100 bill that the CIA dubs their work 'super notes'. They feature flawless engraved images, the same high-tech ink as the genuine article and are printed on the precisely the same mix of 75% cotton and 25% linen.

In Lithuania we also came across perfect US$100 bills but these were attributed to Saddam Hussein, in particular those dated 1988. We took tens of thousands of dollars in payment for timeshare apartments, many of which were 1988 US$100 bills and we never had any problems with the UK banks. But were these bills real or fake? If we had refused them we would have gone out of business because, by now, everyone was paying us in US dollars. My guess is that there are billions of fake US$100 bills still in circulation but to do anything about it would be impossible and pointless. In Vilnius the dollar was king and when you paid in dollars you got a discount.

We had one customer who owned her own bank. She bought US$25,000 worth of timeshares and arrived in our office with two bodyguards. One was carrying a brief case and the other a gun. The case was full of pristine 1988 US$100 dollar bills. The armed bodyguard took out his gun and put it on my desk but closer to him than me. She wore a mink coat and, was *dripping in diamonds and smelling of sherry*. There was no question of us refusing the deal, even though we knew that these notes were more than likely fake. After all, none of our previous transactions had been rejected and we needed the money. This was the largest single deal we did. John bought a Mercedes and I bought a diamond ring for Kasia.

As the weeks went by we attracted more and more wealthy customers who seemed eager to get their cash out of the country in the most legitimate way possible.

Buying a holiday home with undetectable monopoly money seemed a very good way of doing it. We had become their *beautiful launderette*.

The Mafia boys in Lithuania were far more prevalent than those in Poland and were involved in every possible activity. You could spot them a mile off and they loved the attention. Their uniform was a mobile phone, short hair, a polo neck sweater, a red or dark green blazer, dark trousers, highly polished shoes and a BMW or Mercedes Benz motor car. They were highly organised and controlled from Moscow so I was told. They operated in all the Baltic State cities on a sort of franchise basis, were known as Brigades and were, in their eyes, totally above the law. As far as I could see they had four main businesses; alcohol, cigarettes, prostitution and protection. They worked under the umbrella of the 'Baltic News Agency', the BNA, and actually carried business cards. The booze and fags were a smuggling operation and we saw little evidence of that but the protection and prostitution businesses were as open as a golf tournament.

If you started a business in Lithuania you would get a visit from a member of the BNA. Not immediately, as they would first want to see if you were worth a visit. Because we had become their unofficial dry cleaners, we were exempt from any such visit. Once a new business was up and running and was seen to be taking cash then it deserved a special visit. A large black Mercedes or BMW would arrive at the premises and four Brigade Members would invite you to hand over a percentage of your profits. In return they would recommend you to everybody and generally give you all round 'protection', whatever that meant. If you did not agree to pay then you had to be prepared to suffer the consequences. At that time quite a few senior company executives in Moscow were mysteriously disappearing and others had been found with a bullet in the head.

Another popular ruse was to visit, say a chemist, and tell him that they had been paid US$1,000 by a competitor to beat you up and ruin the business and ask him how much he was prepared to pay them not to. It was pointless going to the police. In all my time in Lithuania, I only saw three policemen and they were on traffic duty. In any case, I am sure they were in on the scams as well. Most of these protection rackets went unnoticed but there were two that made a big splash in the local press.

A Chinese restaurant opened in Vilnius and quickly did well as it was the first of its kind in Lithuania. It was packed every lunchtime and evening. Kasia and I used to go there as often as we could because the food was wonderful and we were sick of eating chicken and herrings at home.

One day, the owner had a visit from the BNA, but he declined their kind offer and the next day his kitchen was destroyed by a small explosive device. He patched up his kitchen and was open for business that very same day. He had another visit a few days later from the same men who said that they had heard he had had a spot of trouble. He denied it and said that his kitchen had been slightly damaged by a gas explosion but everything was now fine and he was fully insured anyway.

The following Sunday, Kasia and I went to the Chinese restaurant for lunch. We had our usual delicious feast and left. As we were leaving an old black Volga with no plates came screaming round the corner. It screeched to a halt just underneath one of the restaurant windows. A man wearing a balaclava got out and threw a hand grenade through the window. BANG! There was lots of screaming and people suddenly started pouring out of the restaurant into the street. For a moment I thought we were in a Bond movie and started looking for the crew and cameraman, but this was more like Northern Ireland, it was real.

There were lots of little supermarkets dotted all over Vilnius and the best one by far was IKI. It was owned by a French concern, and had far better choice and quality. Although more expensive and, despite being located on the outskirts of Vilnius, the car park was always full. One day a government official from the Health and Safety department turned up at the store without any warning. He demanded to see the manager and then proceeded to tell him that none of the shelves in the store were coated with the correct fire resistant varnish, and until this matter had been rectified, the store would have to close. As it was a government directive, he did what he was told and went in search for the special varnish. He also did some checking of his own and found out that no other supermarket had been visited nor had special fire resistant varnish on their shelves. Furthermore, he found out that this so called 'special' varnish did not even exist. He went straight round to the government buildings and, after much ferreting, finally dug out the 'varnish' official. The official conceded that the varnish did not exist in Lithuania but he could buy it in Germany. Well this was a load of old bollocks so the manager went to the French Embassy for help. The Ambassador got involved and after a short investigation it was discovered that the whole thing was just another Mafia scam.

The official had been bribed by the Baltic News Agency to close down IKI because it was taking away custom from the supermarkets and shops that they controlled. This incident went to the top and nearly caused an international rift between France and Lithuania, but the BNA backed off and IKI soon re-opened. This scam was a little more sophisticated than chucking hand-grenades through windows, but both demonstrate the lengths that these people were prepared to go to for their much loved dollar.

The Baltic News Agency also ran girls and the operation in Hotel Lietuva was exactly the same as the one in Hotel Poznan. There were a few girls that used to hang around the bars during the day and most of them were very young. We used to sit in the bars during breaks in the afternoon presentations and ogle these Eastern European girls. They were all really very striking, however when any of them smiled you got an instant report on the state of Lithuanian dental hygiene.

The main business was conducted in the evenings from the Panorama Club on the twenty-second floor. These girls were slightly older, had 'Colgate' teeth and were dropped off by their minders at 10:00pm every night. Upstairs in the restaurant, proceedings were controlled by the Madame. She was about twenty-five and blond but I doubt if her collars and cuffs matched. She always wore red hot pants and thigh high patent leather black boots. All the girls had ankle length real mink coats. The Madame sat at her own table from where she could see every other table. Alongside her were usually two or three 'Blazers', as we nicknamed them, again drinking Chivas Regal whisky. The girls would arrive and check in with her. They would then be sent off to go and chat with the expense account business men. At about 11:00pm there was a short cabaret show which involved scantily clad beauties prancing around the dance floor and gyrating to some dreadful music, designed to loosen inhibitions and wallets simultaneously.

One night, after yet another successful presentation, John and I decided to go and have a beer in the Panorama. We watched the show, had another beer and started talking about how we were going to drive the business forward. Suddenly I became aware of a pair of legs next to my left ear. They were a very nice pair of legs. One end disappeared into a pair of leopard skin high heeled shoes and the other end into a very short leather skirt. Uninvited, she sat on my lap, put her arms round my neck and, unlike most of the Polish tarts, spoken very good English.

"I have been looking at you all evening and have decided that I want to have you."

"Well I am very flattered but I'm a happily married man and my wife will be here in a minute." I lied. She immediately glanced over to Madame who came down to see what the trouble was.

"If you do not like this girl I can find you another one, okay?"

"How about you?" I joked.

"You could not afford me, I'm US$300." Not wishing to waste any more time they promptly returned to Headquarters to plan their next assault. John and I went downstairs to get a taxi.

It was blowing a blizzard outside and there was an extensive queue for taxis. To get a taxi the receptionist would call one for you and give you a slip of paper with the registration number so no one else could take your cab. It was a system that worked very well. We had a long wait that night but eventually the receptionist called over to us to let us know that our taxi was on its way. It was freezing and the snow was blowing sideways. We could hardly see anything. Our taxi duly arrived, but as we were about to get in, a Blazer and a girl barged past us. He got in the front and she got in the back. I grabbed hold of the door before he had a chance to close it.

"Hey this is our fucking taxi. Get out!" I shouted and showed him the slip of paper the receptionist had given me. He ignored the slip of paper and tried to close the door which he eventually did. The taxi stood there a few seconds and then he opened the door, smiled and said.

"Get in the back we'll take you home." I opened the back door and there was the girl with her skirt hitched up, legs wide apart with her bush in full view.

"Climb in boys what are you waiting for?" she offered.

I slammed the door we went back inside to order another cab. By the time I got home it was nearly two in the morning and I assumed that Kasia would be worried sick. Quite the opposite, she was fast asleep.

Chapter Nine

Travelling around Vilnius was very straightforward. We were spoilt for choice. Walking was absolutely out of the question for two reasons; firstly, it was far too cold and secondly, it was bloody dangerous. There was three feet of snow everywhere and it was minus twenty all day and minus thirty at night. With the average monthly wage so low the risk of attack was high and there were certain parts of the city that were definite no-go areas for anyone looking like a Western European. The muggers would slit your throat even if they thought you might have fifty bucks on you. So we were left with buses, trolley buses and taxis.

The buses and trolley buses were very frequent and cheap. You could make a journey from one end of Vilnius to the other end for as little as five pence. There were three main problems with this mode of transport. Number one, you could never get on the bus and, if you did, they were always so full you could never get off. Number two, they were always breaking down or crashing and, number three, the ticket inspectors were a bunch of violent madmen. Just like in Poznan you had to buy your book of tickets from a road side kiosk and then have your ticket punched by the little machines that were welded to the inside of the bus doors. However, unlike in Poznan, most of these little machines had been ripped off by vandals or were so badly mangled you could not stick in your ticket.

If you were caught without a ticket the inspectors would just throw you off the bus into the gutter and they did not give a shit if you were a child or a little old lady. They also made no allowance for the lack of serviceable punching machines on the buses. No punched ticket, no travel. One afternoon, three collectors got on my bus and, in-between stops, a fearful argument erupted. At the next stop the inspectors pushed an elderly man off the bus into the snow and then jumped on top of him. They proceeded to kick the shit out of him. When they felt they had dished out enough violence they just got back on the bus and continued to check our tickets.

On another occasion I was traveling on a trolley bus, which is like a normal bus but has no engine. It got its power from overhead electricity cables which frequently broke down. Anyway, I was on this bus and a man got on, pulled out a gun, opened the breech and started filling it with bullets. He then closed the gun, waved it about in the air and shouted at the top of his voice.

"TICKETS."

Fortunately, once we had started to make good money, bus travel was confined to the memory.

Travel by taxi was far quicker, not expensive and highly amusing. There were two types of taxi, the private taxi and the state run radio taxi. The private taxis were a total rip off or tried to be. They were usually old Fiats or Ladas, rarely had meters and, for the most part, unlicensed and hence illegal. They were very easy to spot as their way of advertising was to get an old Tupperware box, paint taxi on it in big red letters and then screw it on to the roof of the car. Bingo! Instant taxi. These were to be avoided at all costs and if the situation ever arose where you had no choice but to take one, then it was advisable to agree a price before departure. One day I found myself in such a situation and I stupidly forgot to negotiate a price. Fortunately my driver was just as stupid, for when we reached my destination and I asked him how much, he just shrugged his shoulders and looked at me with a rather vacuous expression. I gave him five litas and he seemed very happy.

John had a similar experience. He was forced to take one of these private cabs from the bank in the centre of town to the hotel, a distance of about three kilometres. Like me, he totally forgot to set the fare before setting off, so when he got to the hotel he asked the driver how much he had to pay. He too shrugged his shoulders but remembered that he had picked John up from outside a bank, so he blurted out.

"Er… five hundred dollars!" John burst out laughing and after about ten seconds of negotiating, gave him 5 litas and he too, seemed grateful.

The state controlled radio taxis were much better. Most of them were black 1962 Volgas. Model GAZ M-21 Lux. They did have meters but they did not always tell the truth and the seats were always covered in thick nylon fur of varying colours. When I got into my first Volga I noticed that there were no handles to wind the windows down. There was the little cog on to which the handles fitted, but no actual handles. It struck me as being strange. Why does the driver not want me to open the window? Is he frightened I might climb out? Is it to keep out the cold? But then what about the summer? Or do they put them on, on a certain date, a bit like the state run heating system? I could not fathom it out. The next Volga was the same and the next. In fact, none of the Volgas we ever travelled in had handles to wind down the windows. One day I was travelling with Rima in a Volga, so I asked her to ask our driver why.

"They all get stolen." was the reply. This made me even more baffled. What on earth could anybody do with a window handle of a 1962 Volga or even hundreds of them? These cabs did not have any ashtrays either but instead, empty coke cans, cut in half were glued to the inside of the door. Judging by the mess on the door they obviously ripped them off when they were full and glued on another.

These Volga taxi boys were very good drivers and they needed to be as at that time of the year the driving conditions were treacherous. There were mini accidents all the time, but these guys were brilliant at avoiding on-coming traffic and never seemed to lose their cool or control. I remember one evening Kasia and I were going home after a night out and the snow was falling thick and fast. Our Volga driver was in a bit of a hurry. Kasia asked him in Russian to slow down but he ignored her. Give him his due he drove really well and we avoided everything. The road was sheet ice covered in snow and we were sliding all over the place. Suddenly he clipped a curb and the back left passenger door just fell off, bounced down the road and hit the car behind us, causing it to skid and plough straight into a tree. Our driver glanced back momentarily and, despite the sudden blizzard conditions inside the taxi, carried on driving as though nothing had happened.

Chapter Ten

We had had a really shaky start in the business, but I was now making a lot of money. Eating at home became a rarity and there were plenty of surprisingly good restaurants, bars and cafes in Vilnius. McDonald's or Burger King had yet to arrive although it was possible to get a take-away pizza. One day, as a treat, we ordered one for the office staff. It took two hours to arrive, was stone cold and looked like someone had just been sick on a circular piece of cardboard.

The main restaurant in Hotel Lietuva was a vast communist horror and the waiters and waitresses were just as 'friendly and attentive' as the ones in Hotel Poznan. The menu was quite ludicrous. It was about fifty pages long and listed everything from Beluga caviar to chewing gum. However, they very rarely had anything you wanted available. The wine list was exactly the same. The only time you should ever consider going to one of these state restaurants is if everything else is closed and your very existence depends upon immediate sustenance.

I had always loved eating out and experimenting in different restaurants so one day, instead of going to the Chinese, we went to an old, well-established eatery in the middle of the city that we had been advised to go to, not for the food, but for the experience. Their menu was similar to the fifty page job at the hotel. The only things available that day were meatballs and rice and Russian beer. They didn't even have any water. While we were sipping our beer and waiting for the meatballs, we noticed that there were no knives or forks on any of the tables, so we assumed they would arrive with the food.

There were a few other couples in the restaurant and, after a wait of forty-five minutes, our food arrived but no knives or forks. In her best Russian, Kasia asked quite reasonably in a restaurant, if it would be possible if we could have a knife and a fork.

"Oh no, we don't have those; didn't you bring your own?" The waitress replied.

"No. Why should we bring our own cutlery to a restaurant?" Kasia continued.

"Because we don't have any!" she screamed.

"Why?"

She then proceeded to explain that they had not had cutlery items in the restaurant for years as the customers used to get roaring drunk, start fights and use the knives and forks to stab each other.

"Okay," said Kasia, "But how are we going to eat our meatballs and rice now?"

"Use your fingers." And with that she walked off. By now we had lost our appetite and the food had gone cold so we paid the bill and left.

There was, however, one exception to the rule about state restaurants and that was the one in Hotel Turistas, a five minute taxi ride from Hotel Lietuva. The actual hotel was ghastly but on the ground floor there was a very nice looking old fashioned Soviet restaurant. It was run by a tall, attractive woman in her late twenties or early thirties, who spoke good English. She had had extensive formal training in Paris and the food was simple, yet delicious and her menu was the only one in Vilnius that changed daily. The waiters and waitresses were courteous and efficient. The restaurant was always full but they always tried to make room for us and, unlike that over-estimated restaurant on the moon, this one had bags of atmosphere.

There was only one blemish and that was the head waitress. She was an ageing Soviet styled battle-axe. She was fat and ugly and her hair resembled a dollop of mashed potato with dark brown gravy. She was obviously a relic from a time long before this restaurant had been transformed as all she did was waft about trying to flog dead roses from a dilapidated wicker basket. Her other task was to collect money for the excellent jazz band that played at one end of the restaurant. One evening I did not have any small money on me so I asked her to put my band money on the bill.

"No. You must pay me cash now! It is the system!" she screamed. I summoned the manager and pointed out that we were sick of this crotchety old bag as she was always very rude and unpleasant. She had not one redeeming feature. My tirade must have worked as we never saw her again.

Our favourite restaurant was the Artas Kavine Baras. One of the attractions was that it was a two minute walk from our home. It was on the first floor of a block of flats and was quite expensive so it did not attract the riff-raff. It was modern and trendy and played great music, so it became a favourite haunt for a lot of the young professional Lithuanians, including several 'Blazers'. The menu was short and the food good, but the best part for Kasia was the ice cream which she ate by the bucket load.

Kasia and I really missed Studio Jacks, so we asked Rima if there were any really good discos apart from Panorama. She strongly advised us not to go to any other nightclubs in Vilnius.

"If you go and they get even one sniff that you are English you're dead, I promise you." Her view was supported by the *Vilnius, In Your Pocket Guide Book*, which joked, that if you want to try out a night spot, do so with a machine gun.

Shopping in Vilnius was a guinea a minute. There were a few shops, but difficult to find. None of them advertised, so you could walk straight past the shop you had spent hours looking for without realising that the building you had just passed was, in fact, a shop. There was a barely adequate little shopping centre five minutes' walk from our flat. It consisted of a small supermarket, a clothes shop and a grocer. The supermarket food counter stocked very good rye bread, plausible chicken, delicious fresh herring, milk, margarine (no butter) and piles and piles of dried cod. A side of this stuff looked like a badly burned wheel-less skate board and was, no doubt, just as tough. The rest of the supermarket stocked all the usual things like bog rolls and tooth picks. The clothes shop above the supermarket and was very fancy. It seemed totally out of place and was always empty, apart from the bevy of beauties who worked there. I needed a new suit so I thought I'd give them a try. Lo and behold, I found one, a perfect fitting, charcoal grey, 100% cashmere, single breasted suit which was made in England, for the princely sum of US$100.

The grocer was the worst of all. It did not matter what day or time of day you visited the grocer, every piece of fruit or vegetable was always rotten. The only way to find a decent potato or carrot was to buy the whole bloody sack, and if you were lucky, you might find half a dozen that you could use.

The real fun came at the end of a trip to the local supermarket when you had to pay. At that time, all the Lithuanian shops in Vilnius did not have cash registers. They had a drawer under the table and a large brown abacus. When it came to your turn to pay the shop assistant would pick up your goods and flick the beads on the abacus from left to right and back again several times, stare up at the ceiling and then write down the sum you owed on a scrap of paper. The amount of beads flicked, the number of flicks and the quantity of goods never had any correlation whatsoever, but as the money involved was small and it would have been inadvisable to argue, we never questioned this method.

At weekends we would take a taxi to IKI where we could buy Lithuanian fish fingers, without doubt the best in the whole world. Heinz ketchup and excellent cheap Russian champagne was also on offer. When we did eat in, our favourite food was lightly sautéed fresh herrings with mustard sauce and mashed potatoes, washed down with chilled Russian champagne.

There was a huge shopping centre next to Hotel Turistas which reminded me, when age six, of being dragged by my mother to the Kendal Milne department store on Deansgate, Manchester. It was full of junk. The dummy mannequins in the windows were either lying naked on the floor or had ill-fitting 1950s outfits on, lopsided wigs and usually a few toes and fingers were missing. Inside was even worse. At least the dummies in the window displays were, in the main, whole. All of them inside were badly damaged but, the best one by far was a bald, one legged, one eyed woman wearing a short, pleated, tartan skirt and nothing else.

It was that time of the month and Kasia had run out of Always Plus, 'carpets' as we called them. So we set off that Saturday morning in search of a chemist. We found an old state one in the centre and after queuing for ages it was our turn to be served. Kasia spoke to the lady in Russian and explained what she wanted. What the pharmacist did next can be described best like this....If you drive into a service station on most European motorways and want to check the oil level of your engine, there are normally round plastic containers attached to the pillars supporting the forecourt's roof. Inside these containers you can find a roll of green kitchen type paper with a bit sticking out of the bottom. The idea is to pull out and tear off as much as you want. This paper can then be used to unscrew the oil cap and wipe the dipstick, ensuring your hands remain clean at all times.

This pharmacist went to the back of the shop, returning with one of these plastic containers attached to a pole which was mounted on a trolley. She then proceeded to pull out a couple of feet of greyish looking gauze out of its bottom, picked up a pair of dress maker's scissors and said to Kasia.

"How much do you want dear?"

We nearly died laughing. We had vivid visions of thousands upon thousands of Lithuanian girls wrestling with this wretched material every month. We thought that there must be some modern sanitary towels somewhere in Vilnius; after all I certainly could not imagine our fur-coated, bejewelled and ever so glamorous rich banking client fooling around with this stuff twelve times a year. We did eventually find some in a new German Delicatessen. As lovers of Bavarian fare we also bought some bratwurst, bockwurst and a large tin of sauerkraut.

After our '*lederhosen*' lunch we went to see what was on at the cinema. A few weeks before, we had seen *Demolition Man*, with Sylvester Stallone. This was very much a macho man's movie with stacks of gratuitous violence and Kasia did not enjoy it. When we got to the cinema they were showing *Sommersby*, a romantic thriller with Richard Gere and Jodie Foster, a movie we had looked forward to seeing. We bought two tickets, went to a café for a pot of tea, and returned to the cinema in time for the film.

When we sat in our seats I noticed that Kasia was the only woman in the auditorium; the crowd being almost entirely loud-mouthed lads. The film started and it was, of course, *Demolition Man* again. We left the cinema very puzzled and angry. The posters in the cinema all said, '*Sommersby*, now showing'. And the ticket office said the same. Kasia demanded an explanation and was told that they keep reeling out the same film over and over again until people stop coming, irrespective of what is currently being advertised. *Demolition Man* had proved to be very popular, especially with all the young male thugs in Vilnius. Our money was refunded and we walked away disappointed.

On our way home we passed a basement shop. It was nearly 9:00pm so we were very surprised to find it still open. It was a wine shop and had some very beautiful Romanian wine glasses and a selection of some very fine wines. We did not have any nice wine glasses so I decided to buy two and a bottle of decent red wine. Well this proved to be really quite difficult. The shop assistant was leaning over the counter, could not talk, could not walk and was as drunk as a skunk. The security guard wasn't much better. He was slumped in a chair in the corner, clutching an empty bottle of wine. I took two glasses off one of the shelves and put them on the counter.

"I'd like to buy these glasses please," I said. "How much are they?"

"You can't," she slurred. "They are not for sale." At which point she tried to straighten herself and would have fallen over had Kasia not caught her in time. We propped her up against the wall and tried again.

"Look, I want to buy these glasses," I continued. "They must be for sale, after all this is supposed to be a shop isn't it?"

At this point she started to slide down the wall and on her way down she muttered,

"30 litas but they only come in sixes. One glass is 30 litas but you cannot buy one on its own. You have to buy all six and that will cost you 30 litas as well." Kasia was laughing so much she was finding all of this difficult to translate. The moment the assistant had finished babbling she hit the floor and passed out with her head jammed up against a wastepaper basket. Kasia found a roll of brown paper and some carrier bags under the counter. We wrapped these six beautiful glasses very carefully, left 30 litas next to the abacus and headed for the wine department.

In between a large black table and a massive rusty old iron wine rack was another shop assistant equally paralytic. I spotted a bottle of red wine I wanted to buy and pointed it out to her. Unlike her colleague in the glass department this lady was all too keen to help. She spun round like a top, lost her balance and just about managed to grab hold of a corner of the wine rack. She pulled a bottle out and then fell over. She lay face down on the floor for a few minutes, rolled over and then managed to sit up with her back against the wine rack.

"This one?" she mumbled, thrusting the bottle towards me with her head nodding like a toy dog on the back shelf of a 1970s car.

"No. The one above please," I beckoned.

She sighed, grimaced, let the bottle she was holding roll out of her hand and started to climb the rack again. With great determination and a lot of puffing and panting she finally found the right bottle. Now she had to get back to the table, a distance of about ten feet. She cradled the bottle firmly to her bosom, crouched forward slightly, parted her feet to maximise balance and set off. In a few seconds she made it and you could see the relief on her face when she realised that she now had the support of the black table.

Still clutching my bottle she looked at me and said,

"I want money!"

"Fine; how much?"

"I've no idea."

"Well why don't you look at the price tag on the bottle?" I suggested helpfully. She started inspecting the bottle like a monkey looking for fleas on a mate.

She suddenly spotted it and threw her head back in horror.

"This is too expensive," she bleated.

"You are not buying it, I am." I tried to have a look at the bottle myself but she pulled it away.

"You're not getting your hands on this bottle until I've seen the colour of your money, Mister!" I did eventually get to look at the price tag. It was 40 litas, so I pulled the right amount of money out of my wallet and put it on the counter.

She released the bottle in favour of the money and, clutching the notes, slid off the counter into a sozzled heap on the floor.

There were no designer shops in Vilnius and, apart from IKI and the new German delicatessen, all the shops were abacus-wielding ex-communist dinosaurs with very little choice. In addition to these shops there were also lots of markets in and around the city. One glorious, but freezing Saturday morning, we visited a couple and the first one was the Kalvariju market, near the city centre.

The Market Place was huge and in the middle there was a large old building. There was a perimeter fence surrounding the whole area and three hundred stalls had been set up that icy morning, selling anything and everything you could possibly imagine. People had driven in, parked wherever they could and started their own impromptu car boot sale. For some reason the place was crawling with Azerbaijani traders and the ground was a death trap, sheet ice everywhere, liberally sprinkled with snow.

The fixed stalls in the central building were selling fruit, vegetables, clothes, furniture, shoes and looked quite normal. It was the outside traders that really fascinated us. One old Volga had been driven right up against the perimeter fence and the entire car, including the boot was stuffed full of dried cod. You could not have squeezed in one more fish. The trader had a fish in each hand and was waving them around like a turbo-charged windmill, screaming out his prices every ten seconds. On the bonnet of another car a man had laid out for sale various car parts. There was a broken carburetor, a dynamo, six spark plugs, a piston, an old car radio and, perched in the centre of his display, a brand new Barbie Doll still in her original box.

There were little stalls set out all over the place. If the traders didn't have a car bonnet to display their wares, then they would use a chair, a table or a mat laid out on the freezing ground. Most of them were selling old car parts: screws, nuts and bolts, steering wheels, handbrakes, mudguards, windscreens and windscreen wipers and all of these items were either second, third or fourth hand. In fact the only new thing in the whole market was the Barbie Doll.

Suddenly the puzzle that had been niggling me for weeks was instantly solved. The next makeshift stall we came across was a table and on it was a baby's ancient looking light blue bath. In the bathtub there must have been fifty or sixty handles for winding down Volga car windows. I can only assume that the men standing by his stall were Volga taxi drivers buying their handles back. Who else could possibly want them?

There were queues everywhere and the two longest seemed to be heading towards two old petrol tankers. On further inspection, one was dispensing potatoes and the other milk. Sacks hewn out of old clothes were used to carry as many spuds as possible and in the milk queue people were filling up old vodka bottles, medicine bottles and jam jars; in fact any receptacle that would hold liquid.

We discovered that not all queues were queues. There were hundreds of people just standing there in rows holding out their goods. They had not been able to find anywhere to pitch their stall so they just stood there in their ankle length tatty fur coats, fur boots and fur hats, all looking inexorably miserable, hoping someone would buy the goods they had on sale. One elderly woman was selling a very badly knitted *single* sock. Others were peddling live animals which included cats, dogs, white mice, gerbils, chickens, ducks and geese. There was one trader who was holding a huge pig that had defecated all over his coat. He could not put it down as the silly bugger had no leash. We had spent about two hours walking around this staggering place and were extremely cold and mentally shattered. I had never seen so much blatant poverty and desperation in all my life. No wonder families pushed their female offspring into prostitution.

The next market we went to was the Hales Meat Market which was in the middle of the old town. The building looked exactly like the Parthenon in Athens. Inside there were hundreds of stalls, all made of concrete and each one about four foot square, three foot off the ground and had a sloping top surface with a hole in one corner for the blood to drain onto the floor. Every stall was covered in some sort of meat and, as the floor supported no drainage system, there was a constant stream of blood about two inches deep trying to make its way to the exits. The butchers, desperate for business, were vying to out-shout each other and, despite the cold, the smell of rotten carcasses was stomach-churning to say the least. There were no recognisable joints, such as leg of lamb or rib of beef, just chunks of mutilated skinless animal.

On one stall there was half a cow. This poor beast had been hacked from nose to tail and still had her coat on. Her guts and mangled udders were hanging over the side of the stall and when the butcher tried to carve her up even more, we were spattered with blood. Kasia's scream of horror wasn't heard above the din and when I waved frantically at him to stop, he glared at me and threatened the next blow of his meat cleaver would be directed towards me rather than Daisy. We pushed through the crowd and on the next stall there were heads of goats, sheep and pigs. These animals had obviously just been decapitated. Fresh warm blood drained from their necks and they stared as though they were still alive.

My aim was to try and find a nice rib of beef for supper. We finally found a butcher that had not mangled everything in sight and went home with a vaguely familiar piece of meat. I laced it with garlic and red wine and braised it slowly for hours. It was inedible.

The next morning was another glorious day and, as it was Sunday, I went to see if I could find an English newspaper as I had not heard any news from home for ages. Kasia stayed in bed and I took a Volga to Hotel Lietuva. I was in luck. They had a week old *Financial Times* and the previous Thursday's *Guardian*. The bill was an outrageous six dollars.

The two main newspapers in Vilnius were the *Lietuvos Rytas* and the *Respublika*. The *Lietuvos Rytas* was their version of our broadsheets and the *Respublika* was a very aggressive paper that enjoyed scandal and exposing people, including members of the Baltic News Agency. From time to time journalists were found murdered for printing derogatory articles about them.

The editor of this paper had balls. While we were in Vilnius he ran a competition with a US$10,000 prize. It would be awarded to any politician who could come forward and prove that he or she had never taken a bribe or used government funds in any inappropriate way. One did come forward to claim the prize but after some checking it was revealed that he had bought a flat for his mistress. No one else surfaced so the editor upped the prize to US$50,000. I've often thought a competition like this would work in the UK.

Chapter Eleven

The timeshare apartments we sold were in Spain and one of our first customers decided that he wanted to take his wife and two teenage daughters to visit his new holiday home. This threw me a bit, as it was still March and we had not expected anyone wanting to travel until, at the earliest, June. Anyway I told him I'd organise it and let him know. Finding him an apartment for four to six people at the resort on the dates he wanted took ten minutes. The problem was how were we going to get him and his family from Vilnius to Spain?

They needed visas and there was no Spanish Embassy in Lithuania and no Lithuanian Embassy in Spain so how was I going to get him a visa? Then I had a brainwave. I would send his passports to the Lithuanian Embassy in London. They would go to the Spanish Embassy in London, get the visas and then return them to me in Vilnius. This was very convoluted and going to cost US$250. I asked our client to come to the office so I could explain how we were going to work it. He agreed and paid.

To my utter astonishment the plan actually worked and two weeks later they were off to Spain. Not only had they never flown before, but none of them had ever been outside of Vilnius, let alone Lithuania. The flight plans were not simple. They had to fly from Vilnius to Warsaw, Warsaw to Copenhagen and then on to Alicante. To make matters worse, none of them spoke a single word of English or Spanish.

When they got back home, the first thing they did was to come directly to our office. He and his family marched in and sat down in front of me.

"For the first time in my life I have finally witnessed something really worth fighting for: freedom and the freedom to choose. Without you this would have always been a dream beyond my grasp." With that he leaned across the table, grabbed my head in his hands and kissed me on both cheeks. His family queued up and one by one did the same.

Business in Vilnius had dropped off slightly so we decided to look at the possibility of doing a few 'road shows'. The plan was to do one presentation a day in Vilnius on Tuesday, Wednesday and Thursday. On Friday we would hire a bus and driver, head off to some other town with all our staff, set up shop in a hotel and do four presentations, two on Saturday and two on Sunday. All the local businessmen and their families would have already been targeted and invited. On Monday we would pack up and return to Vilnius with squillions of dollars. Well, that was the plan.

We discussed our idea with one of our more worldly-wise customers who recommended we have a look at two other cities, Kaunas and Klaipeda. John jumped in his Mercedes and shot off for a few days to do a reconnaissance of Klaipeda, taking one of the translators. Kasia and I grabbed Romasc to do the same in Kaunas.

Kaunas was a major business centre about one hundred kilometres due west of Vilnius. It had a population then of over 400,000 and just as many dogs. It dated back to the middle of the fourteenth century and was built on the junction of the rivers Neris and Nemunas.

The Old Town covered some hundred odd hectares and was dominated by Gothic and Renaissance styles with a sixteenth century nucleus of merchant houses around the Town Hall. A third of the 545 houses in the old town had already been restored from minor damage received during the Second World War. In fact Kaunas was in far more danger from Soviet style town planners than it had ever been from the Germans since they were currently considering building an eight lane motorway smack through the centre. Sadly, the communists had managed to inflict one eyesore on Kaunas, they had built a huge concrete shoe factory right next to Kaunas Castle.

We needed somewhere central for our presentations, preferably a hotel with some sort of conference facility, so we consulted our Kaunas guide book which pointed us towards another Hotel Lietuva, slap in the centre of town. This was a partially renovated old Soviet hotel, which had also recently taken over the running of the next door Russian style restaurant, the Metropolis. The hotel was like all the other hotels we had seen; bare, bland, basic and boring. However, the restaurant Metropolis was stunning. It was set in a grandiose crimson hall. The carpets were worn but ornate and blood-red in colour. Thick red velvet curtains cascaded from the ceiling and the chairs were Lady Penelope pink, as were the table cloths. It was tatty now and needed lots of TLC, but still magnificent, the sort of place Grandfather would have gone to before the War. This place, at first glance, looked ideal for our purpose so we arranged a meeting with the hotel 'Direktor' the following Friday afternoon at 4:00pm. Before we left we reserved the luxury suite for ourselves.

It was useful that Kasia could communicate in Polish or Russian with the Lithuanians as it meant that we did not have to drag some poor translator round with us. I had demanded that Gold Crown Resorts would pay her, but surprisingly, although he agreed, John did not like this one bit. However, the staff did since Kasia was one of the bosses' girlfriends and it put them at ease.

The next Friday Romasc picked us up early and we took a scenic, leisurely drive to Kaunas. Romasc was very happy with these arrangements as he was being retained by Hotel Lietuva, in Vilnius and paid by us too. He was a great find.

It was yet another bitterly cold but glorious spring morning, and on our way to Kaunas, we made a slight detour to visit a place called Kaisiadoris. We wandered around the town for an hour and that made us a little peckish. We looked for a restaurant for a spot of lunch and eventually found a very old-looking restaurant. It was dark and inside there were large wooden tables and benches, a bit like a school dining room. What made us go in was the wonderful smell emanating from the kitchen. We sat down at one of the tables and were very pleased to see plenty of cutlery, however, all of it was chained to the floor via strategically positioned holes in the tables. There was just about enough slack in each chain to allow you to move the fork from the plate to your mouth. Now we had seen everything. There was no need to ask the waitress why they had chained the cutlery to the floor as we knew it was to ensure that they kept the murder weapons as evidence after fatal stabbings, following drunken brawls.

We arrived at the hotel at about 3:30pm. The receptionist had a moustache and she was wearing a white shirt, a brown tie, a brown double-breasted jacket and knee-length brown shorts. Her feet were shod in white socks and highly polished black lace-ups. Her greasy black hair was cut very short and her large bulbous nose was vodka-red. Her eyes looked as though they were made of opaque glass and her fingernails had been bitten to the hilt. She looked like a tractor in a bad mood.

I leant over the desk and asked her very timidly if she spoke any English. She just glared back at me so Kasia took over.

"We have a reservation for a luxury suite in the name of Miller."

She fumbled through a few pieces of paper on her desk, picked one up, looked at us and shouted: "PASSPORTS!" and stuck out her hand. I gave her our passports which she quickly flicked through and shoved in a drawer under the desk.

"You pay now," she demanded.

"Look lady, we have an appointment at 4:00pm today with your hotel Direktor, so I am not paying you one penny until I have spoken with him and you have returned our passports, understand?"

"The Direktor has gone home," she barked.

"He can't have. I have a fax from him confirming our meeting today." and I showed it to her. She looked at it with little interest, glanced at Kasia and said, "No money, no passports!"

"Dollars or litas?" I replied.

"Only dollars."

So I paid her and she returned our passports and handed us the key to our 'Luxury Suite' No. 241. This suite was on the first floor and cost over US$80 per night, an extortionate amount. Had we both been Lithuanians we would have paid a fifth of that but what the hell, we could afford it and it was, after all, a luxury suite. We had an old king size bed and an en suite avocado coloured bathroom with lashings of mould. Luxurious it was not and the use of the word 'suite' was overly generous to say the least.

By now it was about 6:00pm so we decided to have a stroll around the Old Town. Just as we were leaving the room the telephone rang. It was the Hotel Direktor. He apologised profusely and said he would come to the hotel and meet with us at ten in the morning.

Armed with the guide book we walked down the main precinct in Kaunas towards the city's historic quarter. I lit a cigarette and was immediately arrested as smoking in public was banned. Thanks to Kasia's usual charm offensive, I was let off with a warning. Had I been on my own, I would have, more than likely, let arrogance get the better of me and ended up with a short custodial sentence and/or a huge fine. We continued to the Old Town and found a quaint little café where we sat down and had a drink. The Kaunas guide recommended the Antis Bar and Restaurant for dinner so when we had finished our drinks we set off to find it. This establishment was in a cellar in the old Architect's House with a vaulted hall and painted ceilings. It was charm personified. The only thing that detracted from this place was the old, grey haired, unshaven drunk who was sprawled across the entrance. He was wearing a moth-eaten old greatcoat, bleeding from his mouth and clutching a half open box of matches. As this was a fairly common sight in Eastern Europe and reminded me of Green T-Shirt, I thought nothing more and side stepped him on our way into the restaurant. Kasia suddenly stopped me.

"Rupert, I think he's dead."

"No my darling, he's just passed out. He'll be fine." And we continued into the bar. Despite the décor and the recommendations we felt cold so we had a quick drink there and left to try somewhere else. Our friend was still lying across the entrance so, yet again, we side stepped him and went in search for a place to eat.

"I'm sure he is dead," Kasia said, giving him a once over.

"No he's not," I reassured her and took her by the hand a set off across the square.

We wandered around for about an hour but could not find anything we liked the look of so we returned to the Antis Café. The drunk had, by now, dropped his box of matches and was looking decidedly the worse for wear. Ignoring him we went into the restaurant and had a pretty good dinner. Two hours had passed so we asked for our bill, paid and left. When we got upstairs there was a small crowd standing over Kaunas' answer to Green T-Shirt and a few of them were prodding him with sticks. He was as dead as a dodo.

I felt such a fool. I could have intervened earlier and maybe saved his life but how was I to know he was going to kick the bucket. Anyway I was in Lithuania and getting involved could have had disastrous consequences. Imagine the next day's headlines if one of those prodding him had been a reporter from the local newspaper? 'Rich English capitalist pig robs elderly, sober, law abiding Lithuanian citizen and then slays him'.

Although the hotel brochure in our room indicated that there was a room service facility it more than likely did not exist so we went to the twenty-four hour shop on the corner of the square to stock up with fags, champagne and fruit for Kasia. We were chatting as we entered the shop and the pretty girl behind the counter said.

"Hello, you are English aren't you?"

"Well, yes I am and my fiancée is Polish. Where did you learn English? It's very good."

"Thank you very much. I spent a year and a half working as a nanny for an English family who live in Cornwall."

The three of us carried on chatting for a few minutes and we bought the goods and left the shop. As we were leaving I suddenly remembered about the poor unfortunate deceased drunk who was probably still lying outside the restaurant so I went back inside and explained the situation to this young girl asking if she could call the police and or an ambulance. It was the least we could do. This girl, with whom we had been chatting away with not five minutes earlier, suddenly and without explanation lost all her ability to speak English. She started screaming at me in Lithuanian, ushered me out of the shop which she then closed. We were both dumbfounded. I could only imagine that maybe she sold him his last bottle of vodka and had, therefore, in some way contributed towards his demise?

The next morning the Hotel Direktor was smack on time. He showed us all the hotel facilities and everything seemed perfect for our presentations. There were also plenty of cheap three and four bedroom rooms, which the office staff and sales reps could share. I took notes of all the costs involved and told the Direktor that we would almost certainly take it the following weekend, subject to John's approval. As Romasc was not due to pick us up until four in the afternoon, we went shopping.

Opposite the hotel was a humongous department store called 'Merkurijus'. It was about the only decent shop in Kaunas and stocked everything from frozen French frog's legs to motor cars. I needed some more trousers so we went to the men's department on the third floor.

There were rows and rows of racks of shirts, trousers, jumpers, jackets and suits. Interspersed between these rows were little circular changing booths with green velvet curtains. Unlike English stores there were plenty of young assistants and once you had selected an item you wanted to try on, one of them would take it off you and lead you to one of her booths. Once inside the booth she would hand you the garment and then wait. It was all terribly efficient.

We could not help noticing that the booth next to ours was bulging with people. There must have been at least four women inside the booth. Their assistant, or should I say, accomplice, was was passing lots of clothes into the booth and they were stuffing them inside their coats. Once they had finished they left the booth and waddled down the escalator, passed the security guards, through the main doors and out onto the street. There were no alarm barriers at the exits and nobody batted an eyelid.

By now it was about 1:00pm and we were ravenous. The Kaunas guide book told us that the best restaurant in the city was the Margiris but it was impossible to find. That was an understatement. Although we had excellent directions it took us over an hour. The restaurant was in a large old building standing alone on top of a hill overlooking Kaunas. All the windows were shuttered up and all the doors were closed. The roof was covered in light green moss and the walls dripped with Virginia creeper. The place looked abandoned. There was no sign of life and no advertisement anywhere indicating that this was a restaurant.

Eventually we found a door that opened. We walked down a dimly lit corridor and found another door. Suddenly it opened and a man, wearing a dinner jacket, ushered us in and asked us if we were lunching today? The walls were jet black, the ceiling mirrored and there were no windows. It was entirely lit by hundreds of little candles. We had a delicious roast duck and a bottle of Aloxe Corton 1961. This was a classic example of utter cornucopia amidst total dearth. We could see what motivated the Bolsheviks in 1917.

When we got back to hotel Romasc was waiting for us so we quickly packed and said goodbye to the Direktor. As we were leaving he filled me with optimism for our forthcoming business venture in Kaunas.

"Oh, by the way, if you do decide to bring your business here I strongly recommend you invest in a couple of bodyguards."

I thanked him, but I have always taken a view that if you carry a knife one day you'll be tempted to pull it out, only to find out your adversary has a much bigger one. John's trip to Klaipeda had not been good so we decided to start the road shows in Kaunas. Rima rang the Direktor and we started getting ready to hit Kaunas.

The following Friday morning Kasia, I, Mindaugas and Giedrus jumped into Romasc's car and set off to Kaunas. John would follow with the troops in the bus on Saturday morning. When we got to the hotel our large moustachioed receptionist was a changed woman. She was friendly, very chatty and most welcoming. We were also met by the assistant Direktor who was so enormously fat the folds of skin on her legs almost smothered her shoes. She wasn't interested in seeing our passports and said we could pay at the end. Kasia and I had the same '*luxury suite*' and Giedrus and Mindaugas shared a room next to the bar. We then set up the conference hall for our presentation. It all look great and I was really looking forward to making some good money over the weekend. The response to our invitations had been phenomenal. All four presentations had been oversubscribed which would create exactly the right atmosphere in the hall.

By 7:00pm the preparations were completed so Giedrus and Mindaugas buggered off into town to see if they could get laid and we thought we would try out another recommended place called Vilija. This was on the road out of Kaunas towards Vilnius and dining there also involved a strip show after dinner. We were both up for this so we asked fatty to make a reservation. Vilija was a brightly lit modern building and the car park was full of BMWs which made us slightly apprehensive. We were welcomed by a friendly face, given a complimentary glass of champagne and shown to our table. It reminded me of dining at the Wimbledon dog track in that all the tables were in a semi-circle and you sat next to each other facing the track or, in this case, stage. Virtually everyone else in the joint was BNA or a BNA moll but they did not seem that interested in us although my quintessential English tweed jacket must have made one or two eyebrows twitch.

We had a good dinner and quite a decent bottle of wine but sadly no Aloxe Corton. After the meal we ordered some coffee and cognac and sat back to watch the show. We were expecting some sleazy striptease as that is what the guide book had led us to believe; far from it. What happened over the next two hours was a very classy Crazy Horse Saloon style cabaret performance with a quite brilliant ‘Can-Can’ at the end. According to some recent newspaper articles Vilija was the most dangerous place in Kaunas and to be avoided at all costs.

John and the Gang arrived early the next morning and the first presentation was due to start at 2:00pm. Everyone checked into their shared rooms with the exception of Queen Rima who had a room of her own. After an early lunch everybody got dolled up and at about 1:45pm the prospects started to arrive. They were mainly young couples in their early thirties and all dressed to kill. The women looked fabulous and quite a few had brought their children. One man turned up with two stunning girls who turned out to be his twin daughters. Normally we would never allow in a married person without their spouse as making a decision to buy then and there would be virtually impossible.

This gentleman insisted he be allowed in with his daughters and thank god we did as it was their twenty-first birthday and he bought them one timeshare week each and handed over US$8,000 in cash. Another guy bought two weeks but only had US$3,000, so Mindaugas and I had to go to his office the following Wednesday to pick up the balance. When we got there the place was crawling with minders who frisked us before we were ushered into a back room. In the corner there was a vast bottle-green safe the size of a commercial fridge. When he opened it, it was so full of cash he had to use his knees and arms to stop the carefully bundled wads of notes tumbling to the floor. There and then he decided to buy another two weeks so we left with US$12,500 in cash.

When we got back to the car I instructed Romasc to get out of there as fast as he could.

Another customer was a fish magnate and responsible for all the dried cod in the whole of Eastern Europe. He too paid in cash. They all paid in cash as there was no other way. The reason why these presentations were so successful was that they were done in a small hall to a small audience, no more than eight couples per presentation. Once one had bought and the champagne corks started popping, this fever spread like wildfire.

In four presentations we sold over twenty weeks and took in US$80,000 in cash. Counting the dough in our hotel rooms made us feel like drug dealers and our first weekend road show in Kaunas had surpassed even our wildest dreams so we decided to do it again. The next weekend started off very well but on the Sunday morning a few 'Bandit' Blazers turned up at the Hotel and wanted to know what was going on. A 'Bandit' Blazer was a *rogue* Mafia member and extremely dangerous. John and I hid and Rima took these guys around the presentation room and told them that we were travel agents showing the new way to help people travel abroad. She was very convincing and they left, but she advised that we should get out as soon as possible because if they found out how much money we were taking they would kill us without any question.

Chapter Twelve

Anton and Vanessa were getting married on the seventh of May in England and Kasia and I had been invited. John's brother was getting hitched on the same day, but in America so, as it was around Easter time and we had been very successful, we decided to close the office for two weeks. Rima said she would pop into the office on a daily basis to deal with any matters arising. There was a massive payday coming up and I spent all my time calculating everyone's pay, commissions and bonuses, including mine. Kasia was busy buying wedding presents for Vanessa and Anton, and John was like the king in his counting house counting all the money. It was the best of times.

It was John's franchise. He had the final say on everything and took the largest cut. However, I made many more sales than he did so my payday was going to be very big. One evening John asked me to go for a drink with him after work when he gave me a lovely Swiss watch and US$300 towards our holiday.

"Rupert, this is just to thank you very much for your hard work and input. We are a great team and have a fantastic formula that I hope will generate loads of business for both of us for many years to come."

The next day I completed the pay and bonus figures for the office staff and the commission statements for the sales reps and myself. As usual I gave them to John for final checking and to date I had not made one mistake. The commission due to me was a little over US$8,000, four times what it normally was. John checked the figures; double checked the figures and suddenly asked everyone else to leave the office. And then, without any warning, he set on me; accusing me of cooking the books and stealing from him. He told me I was useless, had done nothing to help and was a total waste of space. He accused Kasia of inciting the staff against him and plotting to overthrow him and steal all his money. I sat him down and tried to show him that the accounts, as always, were faultless and that I was owed every dollar on my commission statement. He was not listening, he was just thinking, "Why should I give Rupert US$8,000? I should keep it myself." He had been inexorably consumed by greed.

I reminded him of our drink and the Swiss watch. He finally agreed that I could pay myself the full amount due.

"Okay, you pay yourself, but I want you to think long and hard. Are you worth it? And, when you realise you're not, I want you to give me most of that money back." Well now I knew he had really flipped. Argument over, the office staff and the sales reps were allowed back in and I paid everyone. That evening Kasia went to see Aida and told her what had happened and she could not believe it. Suddenly there was panic in the ranks because everyone saw that this was the beginning of the end. Nobody wanted a greedy boss.

That weekend we had arranged to do two presentations in a brand new hotel, just outside Vilnius and then on Tuesday we were all off on a much deserved holiday. Hotel Villon was one of the first large private hotels to be built in Lithuania and stood next to two large lakes. Our plan was to do one presentation on Saturday and one on Sunday. The next morning Kasia and I were just getting ready to go to the office when the phone rang.

"Have you thought about how much money you are going to return to me this morning Rupert?"

"Yes John, I have. I am not going to give you back one dime you ungrateful, greedy little arsehole. Understand?"

"Err….. Well… err… I do not want you or Kasia to come to Hotel Villon today. I'm going to do everything myself."

"That's fine by us Woody! We'll go on holiday now and when we come back I seriously hope you have recovered your senses, Goodbye!" and with that I slammed the phone down. Aida rang Kasia later to tell her that John had told the entire staff that I had been stealing from him and I had been sacked. He then issued a warning that, if he had any trouble from anyone else, then he'd make sure they had a special '*visit*'. Well, of course, nobody believed him and, as a result of his massive bout of greed-induced disloyalty, most of the sales reps did not turn up for the Hotel Villon presentations. Both were a total washout. With US$10,000 in our pockets we hopped on the first flight available.

It was race week at Chester and my parents had two spare tickets. One of their friends had suffered a heart attack so we went instead. Chester racecourse, although quite small, was the prettiest I had ever been to and Chester races were always good fun; made even more so by Kasia's scoop on a 33-1 outsider.

After the races were over we said goodbye to my parents and caught a train to London and then another to Windsor where we stayed with my old friend Kathy. The next morning we picked up a hire car and I went to change some Saddam Hussein, 1988 US$100 bills in a bank on the High street. The lady at the foreign exchange counter took my US$3,000, looked at them and then, without saying a word, suddenly disappeared into an office at the back of the bank. A few minutes later a rather stern and important looking man came back with my dollars.

"Do you realise Sir, that these dollar bills have consecutive numbers?"

"Yes I know, I printed them this morning," I joked. He roared with laughter and gave me some genuine, fresh and very crisp, twenty pound notes.

On Saturday it was Anton and Vanessa's big day. After the nuptials, we all went to their house for a sit down lunch for about a hundred people in a marquee on the lawn. Lunch consisted of lobsters and champagne and the speeches were some of the funniest I had heard. By the time it was the turn for the best man's speech, he was so pissed he could barely stand. He eventually got to his feet and started.

"I believe it is customary for the best man to raise a glass and toast the bridesmaids. Well sod them. As the marquee is going to be standing a lot longer than I am, let's drink to the marquee." He then raised his glass, drank its contents and fell flat on his back, out for the count. After the speeches I had a chance to speak to Anton and I told him about the problem with John. Anton had little sympathy for me.

"After all Rupert, most people in the timeshare industry are a bunch of lying, back stabbing, and crooked bastards. I should know."

With our holiday over it was going to be interesting to see if John had recovered from his 'Swamp Fever'. He had not. The keys to our flat did not work so we went to the office but there was nobody there. I tried my keys but the locks had been changed. We returned to our flat and knocked on the landlady's door but there was no reply, so we had no alternative but to break in through the kitchen window. Nothing had been taken from the flat and not only had the locks been changed but they had also put a bloody great bolt and padlock on the inside. John was obviously determined to get rid of me and I was now beginning to wonder how far would he go? He could certainly afford to have Kasia and I disposed of so we decided that we were not going to hang around any longer to find out.

Fortunately the telephone was still working so Kasia rang the airport, but there were no flights, so she tried the station and we were in luck. We had just enough time to pack everything and catch the night train to Warsaw. Also, by taking the train instead of a plane, we would save a packet. Our holiday had been very expensive and we were down to our last US$5,000.

I managed to get hold of Romasc who picked us up and took us to the station. On the way Kasia explained to him what had happened, and Romasc, who was a very gentle giant, got visibly angry and asked me if I would like him to 'offer' Mr. Holmes a spot of violence? If I had said 'yes' John would have been floating down the Neris within the hour. As much as I loathed the spineless little shit I did not want to be branded as an accessory to murder.

We got to the station with our five large cases and were lucky to get a compartment all to ourselves. We spread the luggage over the seats, closed the door and drew the curtains. Each time someone opened the door Kasia just said that we were waiting for our friends. We bade a sad farewell to Romasc who gave me another near fatal bear hug and kissed Kasia. Soon after the train pulled out of Vilnius.

The journey to Poznan via Warsaw was going to take about twenty hours and we would have to travel through Belarus. True to form, our train left on time at 5:30pm and, as soon as it did I went looking for the buffet car but to no avail. Instead, each carriage had an attendant just like the train from Nairobi to Mombassa. However, there was no chance of a gin and tonic with a slice of lemon here. Our carriage had two attendants. One male and one female, both, I imagined, in their mid-twenties. Their job was to issue blankets and tea or coffee. I wanted something stronger to drink but they were strictly an alcohol-free outfit. I thought that there has to be some enterprising attendant on the train running a little sideline so I went in search of him. Sure enough, at the far end of the train, one guard was selling beer and biscuits. We had not eaten since the flight that morning so I bought all his biscuits and half a dozen cans of beer. We drank some beer, ate the biscuits and settled down for the long night ahead.

At about one in the morning we arrived at the Belarus border. The train stopped and we knew that we would have a long wait while they checked everybody. They eventually got to our compartment. There was a Polish official, two Belorussian officials and a Belorussian customs officer. All wore really filthy green uniforms and peaked caps very similar to those worn by members of the North Korean armed forces. In addition, their whiffy body odour was exacerbated by cheap deodorant.

"PASSPORTS!" The familiar demand.

We handed them over and they took one brief look at Kasia's passport and then handed it straight back. They looked at mine and then looked at me. He then opened my passport at the photograph page and held it up next to my face. They started muttering to each other and shook their heads. In the last twelve months I had lost about three stone in weight. I no longer resembled the porky pig in the passport. They were not convinced it was me. Kasia came to the rescue again and started telling the Polish official that it was me and that I had been ill and had lost weight. She really laid it on thick with her charm and smile. They eventually stamped my passport and were about to give it back when the Belorussian customs officer stepped forward, took my passport and put it in his pocket. We had five large cases but he was not in the slightest bit interested in them.

"You need a transit visa." he said.

"No I do not. We checked at the station. Give me back my passport please."

He then pushed passed Kasia, opened the window and called out to some of his colleagues who were standing on the platform. Two of them then ran onto the train arrested me, handcuffed me and marched me off the train over to a large building. I was dragged up three flights of stairs, released from my handcuffs and locked in a room no bigger than a broom cupboard. I thought, '*shit they are going to kill me*'.

The Belorussian customs officers had a simple rule. If they thought you may have some US dollars on you then you would require an expensive transit visa and if they did not then you wouldn't. I had five thousand dollars on me plus a Scottish twenty pound note. I was petrified, the train was about to leave and I was stuck in this little room. Furthermore, Kasia was on the train and had not got a bean on her. I took all but a one hundred dollar bill (1988) and the Scottish twenty pound note out of my wallet and buried the money beneath my balls.

Shortly afterwards the door to my cell opened and I was taken to a little office, where a very large woman was sitting behind a desk. She had oily dark hair tied up into a bun and piles of dandruff had congregated all over the shoulders of her equally disgusting green uniform. On the desk was my passport so I felt a little calmer and I could also see the train out of the window. They were jacking it up to change the wheels as the track gauge in Lithuania was different to Belarus and Poland. I suddenly felt a great sense of relief as this was going to take hours.

"You have dollars, yes? You must pay for visa." she growled.

I took my wallet out of my pocket and pulled out the Scottish twenty pound note and put it on the table.

"Okay?" I asked nervously.

One of the guards in the room took one look at this unfamiliar note on the table, pulled his gun out of it's holster and, pointing it at my head, screamed,

"Dollars NOW!" And he went bright red in the face. I was convinced he was about to pull the trigger. To make the situation worse, I could feel the wad of notes nestling under my balls begin to move. This was not good. I picked up the Scottish note and replaced it with the hundred dollar bill I had kept in my wallet. This did the trick as the guard put his gun back into his holster and they all started to smile. Albeit an encouraging sign I still needed to do something urgently about the dollars in my boxer shorts. Why, oh why was I not wearing 'Y' fronts!

If those guys had started to see dollar bills appear from the bottom of my trousers they would have nicked the lot and I would have been fed to the pigs. I had to get out of the room as quickly as possible, so I crossed my legs and said.

"Toilet?" I was escorted down the corridor. Thank god I had drunk a few beers earlier so I did actually need a piss because standing in a toilet not doing anything would have certainly aroused their suspicions. As they had all smiled when I put the dollar bill on the desk I thought it unlikely that they would search me, so I rescued my wad of notes, which was now a bit smelly and then split it into four equal mini-wads and put one in each pocket.

When I got back to the office the Saddam Hussein bill had vanished and Mrs. Snowyshoulders was holding my passport. She glared at me, handed over my passport and, with a wave of her hand, indicated that I was free to go. I turned round very slowly and walked towards the door. When I got inside the corridor my pace quickened and by the time I had reached the stairs I was running. I leapt down all three flights, ran out of the building and raced to the train. Kasia was leaning out of the window and the moment she saw me her faced broke into a wide smile. I got to the compartment and hugged her half to death.

"I thought I was never going to see you again." she said and burst into tears.

"I thought I was never going to see me again either," I joked and then we both collapsed onto the seats and roared with laughter.

I suddenly realised that, in my haste to get out of that hell hole as quickly as possible, I had not checked to see if they had stamped my passport with a transit visa. I quickly flicked through it but found nothing. I just hoped that they'd get caught trying to spend a Saddam Hussain hundred dollar bill. The engineers finished changing the wheels and half an hour later we sailed through the Polish border without any problems and were soon steaming towards Warsaw. We put our heads down and quickly fell asleep.

At 6:00am the train pulled into a siding just outside Bialystok. I woke up. It was a lovely sunny morning so I went in search of some coffee but could not find our attendants. Kasia was still fast asleep. I opened the window, leant out and lit a cigarette. There was a funny noise coming from underneath the train. It wasn't a 'train' type of noise; it was more of a human scuffling sort of noise. A few minutes later our male attendant appeared from under the train carrying two large black bags and, opening the door, handed them to his female accomplice. He then disappeared under the train again and retrieved two more bags. This happened another three times and then he spotted me. They immediately abandoned what they were doing and locked themselves in their compartment. I decided to investigate so I knocked on their door. At first there was no answer but I knew they were in there so I knocked again, but much harder. The door slowly opened and I was invited in. There were eight large black hold-alls in the compartment and the two attendants looked extremely shifty. The female attendant unzipped one of the bags and pulled out two cartons of Marlboro cigarettes and handed them to me. They knew I was English and that I had been 'interviewed' at the border, so rather than get aggressive with me and risk me reporting them, they had thought that a bribe was going to be better. They were right and I returned to our compartment with my contraband.

A few minutes later the train started to move again so I lay down on the seat and went back to sleep. At about

9:00am we suddenly woke with a jolt so looked out of the window to see where we were. We had arrived at Zielonka, a district of Warsaw on the east side of the city. We were both ravenous and longed for a coffee so I went to see if I could get some victuals from our attendants but when I got to their compartment both they and the cigarettes had vanished. There was a guard walking down the platform so Kasia pulled the window down and asked him how long the train was going to stay there for?

"Twenty minutes." He replied.

Plenty of time to go and get some food from the station so, armed with a hundred dollar bill, Kasia went in search of a Kantor and some much needed breakfast. I leant out of the window, lit a fag and started to reflect upon the events of the past twenty four hours. I began to daydream when suddenly the train started to move. It couldn't have been twenty minutes since we stopped, more like about five so I checked my watch. I was right; it had been less than five minutes. Panic set in immediately. I jumped off the train and ran up and down the platform, waving my arms about frenetically, screaming at the top of my voice.

"Stop the fucking train. Someone has stolen my wife." I made such a noise that one of the platform guards signalled ahead and the train did actually stop. A few guards approached me and with my limited Polish and a bit of acting I managed to convey to them what had happened and they set off to look for Kasia. I had just about calmed down when the train started moving again. Luckily our carriage window was still open and I was standing on the platform next to it. Without hesitation I grabbed hold of the top part of the lowered window and started to haul myself up. One of the guards saw this and ran over to try and pull me off. I pushed him away and told him to stop the train right now. It could not leave the station with a man hanging out of a window so they complied. At that moment Kasia appeared, clutching two hamburgers and some coffee.

"Oh my god. What's going on?" A perfectly reasonable question in the circumstances I thought so I explained over breakfast.

While we were still eating our greasy hamburgers we had a visit from the train inspector who, for some odd reason, wanted to interview Kasia about the train stopping incident but wanted her alone and asked her to accompany him to the guards van. I followed them down the corridor but he turned round and attempted to shoo me away. I asked Kasia to make it very clear to him that any interview was going to include me.

We sat down in the guards van and he began to explain that each time a train braked it cost one million eight hundred thousand zlotys, about fifty quid and, as we had caused the train to unnecessarily brake twice, we had to pay three million six hundred thousand zlotys. Furthermore, if we paid him now, he'd knock a bit off. I lost my temper. I was sick of being ripped off by border guards, customs officers, taxi drivers and train inspectors. I stood up and screamed at him and told him he could take his brake story and shove it up his fucking arse! Kasia did not need to translate this bit. I also made it clear to him that if we did owe the railway any money then we would pay it when we got off the train in Poznan and that a receipt would be required. Moreover, I suggested that I might report him to the police for attempted extortion. This really put the heebie-jeebies up him and he started to sweat rather profusely.

I grabbed Kasia by the hand and we returned to our compartment. Half an hour later the inspector came to see us again. He was shaking like a leaf. This time he apologised unreservedly and said something about the driver making a silly mistake and it wasn't our fault that the train had had to brake and he was very sorry for any inconvenience caused. I wasn't really interested in his pathetic little sob story as we were getting very close to Poznan. We arrived at 12:30pm, exactly nineteen hours after we had left Vilnius. We were both, thirsty, hungry, dirty and exhausted. But we were home.

Chapter Thirteen

It was now the middle of May 1994 and I had been in Eastern Europe for almost exactly one year. I had lost three stone in weight, gained the most beautiful girl in the world, got no job, and only five thousand dollars in my pocket. What was I going to do? Well, for the summer, absolutely nothing. We just bummed around spending money. To be honest I was quite glad just to be alive and did not miss working at all. I knew the money was not going to last long and I would have to find something to do, but for now we were just going to chill out. There was no question of going back to the UK as I was virtually unemployable and Kasia wanted to be close to her family. In addition, what money we had would last a hell of a lot longer in Poland.

Apart from reading a great deal we used to go for long walks and when the weather was nice we would cycle to the lake at Strzeszynek and go swimming. Strzeszynek was a natural lake surrounded by forests and in front of it was a large open field where Poznanians would congregate to sunbathe and swim. Dotted round the edge of this field were cafes, bars and ice cream vendors so you could spend a very pleasant day down by the lake.

Poland, unlike the UK, has very distinct seasons. Winter is cold and snowy, spring is bright and cool; summer is long and hot and autumn is crisp and dry. The summer of 1994 was very lazy and very hazy and by the end of it we were running out of money so we had to put our thinking caps on. I sent a letter to Anton explaining that we were now back in Poznan and asked if he had got anything else going on in this neck of the woods. He replied saying that he did not but what we could do was to write to all the existing Polish customers and offer them another timeshare week but at a fifth of the price. He would provide all the addresses and the marketing material and all I had to do was find a computer and write the letters.

One of Luiza's friends father was self-employed and lived on the way to the lake. He had a computer which he let me borrow for nothing. I got started straight away and within a few days I had mailed all the old Polish customers in the Wielkopolska District. I had an instant response but not the one I had anticipated. Those that contacted me were absolutely furious and demanded their money back immediately. I had no idea what they were talking about until one of them agreed to see me without killing me. Just in case, we took Kasia's brother, Zbigniew with us.

The customer was quite calm and explained what had been going on. After Anton had sacked the two Serbs they had kept all the names and addresses and Bojana had been offering the customers bogus holidays and free flights to Spain. They had taken stacks of deposits off the customers and then buggered off back to Belgrade with all the money. They were wanted by the police and this customer recommended I contact the lawyer dealing with the matter, a certain Artur Borek.

I reported this back to Anton who wrote to every aggrieved Pole offering full compensation and sincere apologies. Anton also sent me £1,000 for my trouble. By now we were skint so this cash saved our bacon.

I went see Artur Borek who had actually bought a timeshare off the Serbs before I had arrived in Poznan. I assured him that I had nothing to do with this scam and that Anton would make good all the damage. Borek spoke a little English but asked me if I would teach him professionally. I wasn't a teacher. How could I teach? I knew nothing about it. He told me that there was a huge demand for native speakers teaching English privately and that I should put an advert in the Poznan paper offering my services. We did not have a telephone so in the advert we invited interested parties to come to the flat. A few did and then I got some referrals and in no time at all I was up to fifteen hours a week at 150,000 zloty per hour, a living wage in Poznan. Most of my clients were students whose parents paid and I had Borek who paid me monthly in advance. One of my clients was the lady in charge of the Polish national swimming team and wanted to learn English in preparation for the 1996 Olympic Games in Atlanta. She could not speak one word of English but was quite happy to pay me handsomely just to read to her twice a week.

My teaching method was not very orthodox and to help make it more interesting my textbook was the *Daily Telegraph* which I could now buy from Hotel Poznan. Apart from picking up and speaking English for an hour or so each week, they also found out what was going on in the rest of the world. Maybe I should have charged them for the current affairs lesson too?

Kasia's English was excellent now and Borek asked me if she would like to teach his children basic English as, although English was now being taught in the schools, the standard was not very good because there was still a lack of adequately trained teachers. She agreed and was soon teaching some of Borek's clients children as well. Borek had a few *'special'* clients that would have belonged to the BNA had they lived in Lithuania. He had one client who drove a gold BMW 635Csi. He was tall, tanned, very muscular and had had his head shaved. He used to pick Kasia up outside our flat, take her to his home where she taught his two little girls and then drove her back. One evening when he dropped her off he said.

"If you and Rupert ever have any trouble just let me know okay?"

Three of Kasia's clients were the small children of a Mr. Grzegorz Kowalczyk, another of Borek's clients but an '*unspecial*' one. Grzegorz, his wife Ewa and their children, Marcin, Jacek and Marta lived in Plewiska, a suburb of Poznan on the south west side of the city. One evening Kasia came back from teaching the Kowalczyk children. She said that Grzegorz wanted to discuss the possibility of me working for him and could I go and see him as soon as possible. The next day, after my lessons, I hopped on the No. 13 tram and went to go and see him in his office on Ul.Miczurina in the Grunwald district of Poznan.

The name of the company was Komax Sp. z o.o. (Ltd). It was a new office block and they occupied a few rooms on the ground floor. The first person I met was Ela, an elegant woman in her late thirties, who was the company accountant and finance director.

"Hi I'm Rupert Miller; I've come to see Grzegorz Kowalczyk."

"Please take a seat. I'll tell him you are here."

"You speak good English."

"Thank you. You are very kind but it is only limited."

A few minutes later Ela returned with Grzegorz who was short, moustachioed and casually dressed. All three of us went into his office and then, with Ela trying to translate, Grzegorz started telling me all about Komax and what he now wanted to do and why he thought I may be able to help him achieve his goals.

After the Berlin wall came down in 1989 people in Poland were desperate to get their hands on modern western technology such as computers and printers so they could start trading with the West. If you wanted to trade with Russia you had to drive through Poland and, therefore, the opportunities for new ventures here were enormous. Many new entrepreneurs started buying Hewlet-Packard, Canon and Epson printers; to name a few. A printer needs paper and so Grzegorz and his brother, Jacek started importing computer paper from Berlin. They hired huge trucks and drove them through the night picking up the paper then driving back to Poznan adding on a 150% mark-up.

They did this for a year but couldn't meet the demand so they decided to manufacture their own paper in Poland. With the money they had made and with some finance from a third party, Jerzy Kuc, they bought an old building in Kuc's hometown of Grudziadz, a three hour drive from Poznan. They then acquired secondhand machines from Italy and started converting jumbo rolls, imported from a company called Hauffe in Germany, into computer paper. This they then sold all over Poland.

Komax had also started importing computer accessories such as ink jet cartridges, toner cartridges and ribbon cassettes, but Grzegorz had two major problems. The first was that the massive increase in the supply of computer paper had reduced his operating profit from 150% down to about 18%. Although it was still a good business he needed to expand his areas of interest. The second was the ever increasing demand for computer accessories - everything from a simple Hewlett-Packard ink jet cartridge to a mouse pad – made him over-reliant on his one supplier, Despec Supplies in Holland.

Komax sold the computer paper and the accessories to retailers who always wanted credit and thirty days to pay. In order for the system to work, Komax had to have a credit facility with its suppliers and thirty days or more, to pay too. The credit limit with Despec was only US$20,000 which meant that Grzegorz was missing out on a stack of business. That's where I came in.

I did not want to jump in with all fours, as it might not have worked, and I needed to protect my teaching income, so I suggested to Grzegorz that I could start part-time and see how it panned out. The following Monday I went to Komax for my first day's work. When I arrived they were all in a meeting discussing the events of the recent Poznan Computer Fair where Komax had had a stand. I was formally introduced to everyone, including Jacek, Grzegorz's younger brother who ran the office of Komax I, the main distributor for Komax. Komax I was housed in a long wooden hut in Plewiska near to where the brothers lived.

Grzegorz then took me to another office where Piotr Konieczny, the sales manager sat. Piotr was a bit younger than me. He was not as tall, fairly chubby but had a friendly smile. He was very enthusiastic, like most Poles, and although he spoke no English we got on like a house on fire. Somehow we managed to communicate. Grzegorz gave me a thick book which listed every single computer orientated company in the world.

"Find me suppliers okay?" He said in his very broken English. The first thing I did was to sit down with Piotr and Ela and get details of all the potential products and prioritise them. Now I had to find companies that supplied the stuff. At this stage Piotr wanted to purchase as many HP inkjet cartridges, HP Toners, Epson inkjets, Canon bubble jet and OKI ribbon cassettes as he could and said he could easily sell US$100,000 worth of these products monthly. Given the speed of which the market was changing and the threat of competition, it was essential to find suppliers quickly and those with '*very good prices for Polish pocket*'.

A few days later I rang a company called Peacock in Germany and spoke to Ingrid Beller. Ingrid had the sexiest voice I had ever heard and I had visions of this gorgeous pouting fraulein lying naked on a chaise longue. Peacock had all the accessories we wanted so I got Piotr to put together a preliminary order which I faxed to Ingrid. Ingrid's prices were very acceptable but now it was a question of the credit.

"Rupert, my boss says you can have a US$10,000 credit facility to start with." she informed me in her sexy dulcet tones and I started to dream about how gorgeous she must be.

"Ingrid that is no good to us at all. We need at least US$75,000, preferably US$100,000 please and we need it now."

"Rupert it is impossible, but I will see what I can do for you," she oozed down the telephone line. She was on our side as she was paid a commission on what I bought. I helped by faxing to her all the Komax articles of association, bank details, references and I even faxed over my *enriched* Curriculum Vitae. After more calls and faxes we finally got a credit limit of US$50,000 and thirty days to pay. Grzegorz was over the moon. On the first due date we paid Peacock smack on time and they increased the limit to US$75,000 but would not go any higher.

So we now had two suppliers, Despec and Peacock but we needed more as the demand for these accessories was increasing expeditiously. The next company I tried was a supplier called ISA France, based in Paris. They would not play ball so I persuaded the two young bosses to come over to Poland. Grzegorz and I met them at the airport and took them back to the office in his brand new 3 litre Honda. They were quite bewildered as they really thought that they were coming to a one horse town where the horse had died. They could not believe that we had cars, let alone computers. They stayed a few days and we took them to the Palladium night club and made sure they were well entertained and a few days later, surprise, surprise we got what we wanted.

Over the next few months I added ISA Germany, UFP France and Daisytek USA, to our portfolio of suppliers and in total we had nearly US$200,000 worth of credit. Grzegorz invited Kasia and I to join him and his family on a long weekend in Miedzyzdroje, a seaside resort on the Baltic coast. During the weekend we drank a great deal of vodka and I agreed to work full-time for Komax.

The first thing we needed was a really well organised storeman as, apart from all the stuff we were importing from the likes of Peacock, ISA France, ISA Germany, UFP, Despec Supplies and Daisytek, we were also importing compatibles from Keymax in the UK and keyboards, speakers, mice, mouse pads and cleaning equipment from Addison in Holland. I had recently met a young Pole called Piotr Pudliszewski in our local Drink Bar. He was very amenable and looking for a job. He was well educated and spoke reasonable English. Both Kasia and I liked him immediately and so did Grzegorz.

The other two recruitments were Radek Nowak, a design and marketing graduate and Katarzyna Ozog, a rather pretty but dizzy redhead. I was never sure why she was employed and nor was Ela. Ozog used to turn up for work wearing see-through very short dresses, skimpy knickers and no bra. Ela was constantly reminding her that this was a place of work not a bordello. Ozog just ignored her.

In October 1995 Kasia suddenly announced that she was pregnant. Wow. I was going to become a dad. I was totally ecstatic, in fact we both were. It was the best possible news. It put a real spring in my step and I felt I could do anything. Brilliant; just fucking brilliant! I cannot remember being happier and even Jules' death seemed like a distant memory. Life was sweet again.

Over the past few months the computer accessory part of the business had become far more important than computer paper and Mr Jerzy Kuc was not pleased as he saw me as a threat to his control in Komax. Kuc was considerably older than Grzegorz and was very much of the old communist brigade. He was a large man with slick black hair (and not much of it) and he started coming down from Grudziadz to Poznan more often. He wandered around complaining about everything but, as he was the majority shareholder, he had that entitlement. Kuc was like the Fat Controller from Thomas the Tank Engine. He thought that he could just sit in his Ivory Tower and let Grzegorz do all the work. Grzegorz, however, had plans of his own.

The Polish Government had passed a law recently which stipulated that by 1996 every sale made in any shop must be recorded on a piece of paper with carbon copies for the VAT man and the Inland Revenue. In preparation, IT companies started importing electronic cash registers but, with his experience in the paper industry, Grzegorz decided that he was going to become the largest manufacturer of till rolls in Poland.

His other plan was to transfer all the computer accessory business over to Komax I, which was wholly owned by Grzegorz and his brother Jacek. Jacek was very laid back and was quite happy to let Grzegorz have total control. There was no sibling rivalry. I rang all our suppliers, explained the position and in one fell swoop all the credit lines were transferred from Komax to Komax I.

The next weekend Radek removed the hard drive from my computer and installed it in my one at Komax I. The following Monday morning, Piotr Konieczny, Radek, Piotr Pudliszewski and I resigned from Komax, got into Konieczny's car and drove round to Komax I where we started trading immediately. Ozog left the company to get married and Ela, for the time being, remained as our spy

Komax still had the computer paper manufacturing business but Grzegorz controlled all the distribution outlets so Kuc had to keep making the stuff and supplying Komax I. I controlled all the importing and so everyone had plenty to sell. Rafal Kasubiak was the Komax I sales manager and a young girl named Agnieszka did the accounts. Grzegorz's mother was always popping in with baskets full of cakes and whenever it was anybody's birthday or name day, work stopped early and the desks were cleared. Trays of cakes and biscuits would arrive, followed by hams, sausages, beer and, of course, the ubiquitous vodka.

The long wooden hut that was the office of Komax I was on one side of Wolczynska Street and, on the other side, was a plot the size of a football pitch owned by Grzegorz's parents. It was on this land that Grzegorz planned to build his new cash register roll business in time for the 1996 deadline. To build the offices and factory, he needed to raise US$250,000 and he started to write his business plan. His idea was to set up a joint venture company, Emu Sp. z o.o. (Ltd). Komax I would own 51%, Mitsui Hamburg 29% and Hauffe, Germany, 20%.

Grzegorz had been in contact with Mitsui for years and Hauffe had been supplying Komax with jumbo paper rolls since he started manufacturing in Grudziadz. Mitsui was and still is an enormous organisation which turned over one hundred billion dollars' worth of transactions every year and employed over thirty six thousand people in seventy-five countries.

When Grzegorz had finished his business plan he hired a professional to translate it into English. It was then my job to interpret the translation so it would be far more readable and persuasive. After all, he was trying to get a bunch of Japanese to stump up a whole pile of cash so he could make till rolls in Poland, and he knew that without Mitsui the venture wouldn't work.

If you translate directly from Polish into English you invariably end up with double-Dutch so trying to deal with Grzegorz's business plan was very difficult. It was a bit like Chinese whispers. I would sit down with the translator, Grzegorz, and Ela and get her to translate a paragraph. I would then ask Ela and Grzegorz to explain to me what they were trying to say. I would then put that into my own words on the computer and read it back to the translator who would then tell Grzegorz and Ela what I had written.

Sometimes we got it the first time and other times it needed plenty of tweaking. This took about a week. We started at 8:00am and some nights I did not get home until two or three the next morning. We finally finished and copies of the business plan were then beautifully bound and sent by courier to Hauffe in Germany and to Mitsui's head office in Tokyo.

The plan worked and we prepared for some very senior Japanese Mitsui directors to arrive to finalise Emu Sp. z o.o. Hauffe were not instrumental as they had said all along that if Mitsui were in then so were they. The directors arrived and we put them up in the Green Hotel, a brand new small, luxury hotel in the country about ten minutes' drive from the office. The Japanese brought their own translators so all meetings were held in Japanese/Polish. They were with us four days and, apart from inspecting all the paperwork, banking arrangements and building sites, we also had to entertain them every night. It was exhausting. Grzegorz with Ewa, Jacek with his wife also named Kasia, Kasia and I, the three Mitsui directors and two translators were the group. Unfortunately the translators spoke quite passable English so I always had to sit next to one. At dinner, talking to them was like trying to get an MP to discuss his expense claims.

"Mr. Yaimichi, are you married?"

"Yes."

"Does your wife work?"

"No."

"What does she do?"

"Clean house all day."

I wasn't getting very far so I tried another tack.

"What music do you like?"

"Only Mitsui Company Song." And he then started to hum a few bars.

I could see that the others were not faring any better, so dinners were a question of eating as quickly as possible and getting them back to the Green Hotel. During dinner they never drank anything but water and slightly frowned on us for getting stuck in, but we found out later from the Green Hotel manager that, when we dropped them off, these sly little buggers had arranged for bottles of Johnny Walker Black Label to be delivered to the hotel, plus a girl or two, to 'love them in their rooms'.

So the deal was done and, as it was now nearly Christmas, it was important to get the factory built as soon as possible, the Italian machinery installed and the production started. Piotr Pudliszewski was promoted to salesman, a job he proved to be very good at and soon had some major accounts. By Easter 1996 most of the new office block had been completed and Ela left Kuc at Komax. As Kasia had accepted my proposal of marriage ages ago and my decree absolute had arrived, we decided to get married before the baby arrived. We had a quiet civil ceremony in Poznan town hall and a reception lunch at the Chinese, followed by a few days' honeymoon in Krakow.

All the imports of computer accessories were running smoothly and mostly automated by now so I found myself with not much on my plate. Grzegorz was always looking for new lines of credit so I was dispatched to the CeBIT International Computer Fair in Hanover, North Germany. Apart from trying to get new suppliers I also had an opportunity to meet my existing suppliers, especially the gorgeous sounding Ingrid Beller. When I met her I had that same stomach churning feeling I had when I saw that my name had *not* been included in the Dragon School 1stXI cricket team. As for the extra credit, I came away empty-handed.

Plewiska was a tiny village which consisted of about two hundred houses, three or four dirt track roads, no pavements, one general store and a little Drink Bar. We used this bar as our unofficial boardroom. One day Grzegorz and I were having a beer and discussed the possibility of other suitable things to import for the Polish market. He asked me to put my thinking cap on and formed Mex SA, 50% owned by Grzegorz and 50% by my new wife, to deal with whatever products I considered salesworthy.

I began to look at the whole market very carefully and I noticed that there was very little for the ladies to drink as a cheap, everyday alcoholic beverage. For the men there was an abundance of beer or vodka. Wine was still in its infancy in Poland, and when the girls did go out, they would drink expensive cocktails. To some extent, the current situation mirrored the British drink scene in the early 50s and 60s; not much choice for the girls.

Considering Britain as my model, I remembered that in 1953 Francis Showering invented and launched Babycham in the UK. For twenty years it proved very popular and I thought that it would be perfect for the Polish market. The only person I knew in the catering trade in England was Mike Porter, whose family used to run the Bear Hotel at Woodstock, next to Blenheim Palace. I decided to ring him and ask if he could find out if Babycham still existed and, if it did, who made it.

Michael put me in touch with Matthew Clarke who was then the distributor of Babycham. After a few phone calls twenty-four bottles of Babycham were couriered to Plewiska. We had a little tasting session in the office and all the girls said it was lovely and they would buy it, but what was it going to cost? This was where we encountered the first problem. Apart from the cost of the product we had to add on the shipping, import duty, VAT and luxury tax before our profit. The luxury tax was imposed by the Polish government to encourage Poles to drink alcohol produced in Poland as breweries and distilleries were major employers. The luxury tax made the Babycham project unviable. I returned to the drawing board.

In the meantime, Kasia was nearing the end of the pregnancy and we did not care if it was a boy or a girl. However, during one of her visits to hospital, Kasia was told after her ultrasound scan, to expect a girl, so plans were made for a nice little pink cot with lots of girly pink clothes. We had also decided on a name: Patricia, pronounced *Patritzia* in Polish. She got fatter and fatter and the due date drew closer. On Monday, the twenty-ninth of July 1996 at 4:00am, we rushed to the hospital. I was shown to a waiting room and Kasia was wheeled off on a bed. I asked the nurse, who spoke a little English, what was going on and I told her that I wanted to be at the birth.

"Please. No worry. Only now look. They back soon." I sat down and waited. Sure enough they did come back and left me and Kasia in the room together. She was on the bed wearing a rather unflattering maternity frock. Suddenly a doctor and a nurse rushed in started blabbering to Kasia and then wheeled her out. As she left she cried, "There is a problem; they are going to cut me open." They then disappeared into the operating theatre and I was ushered back into the waiting room. Ten minutes later the nurse popped her head round the door and smiled.

"Come and see your son."

"Son? It's supposed to be a girl."

I went into the theatre and got the shock of my life. My beautiful wife was lying on this table opened up and covered in blood. She reminded me of that butchered cow in Vilnius. The doctor was holding up a bright purple skinned rabbit upside down.

"This is your son. Apart from the fact that he is not breathing the X-ray shows he has a serious spinal problem and you can see that his right hand is deformed."

I was finding this all very difficult to take in and I had to sit down. The doctor suddenly got this little thing to show some signs of life and both my son and his mother were whisked away. I was left in total shock and was convinced that they were both dead, so I went to try and find out. I wandered around the hospital for about half an hour until I did manage to get some information. Kasia had been stitched up and was heavily sedated but was fine and our son was in intensive care. I was advised not to come back until the afternoon.

I took a taxi to the office and rang my parents. They were devastated and offered to come over, but my father had not been too well recently, so that was not a good idea. Grzegorz was sweet. He gave me a big hug and stuffed a bundle of notes in my top pocket. Then he drove me to Wuthering Heights where I broke the news to Kasia's family. Her mother was beside herself with worry. This was her first grandchild. What could possibly have gone wrong? We went to the hospital at 2:00pm and I went in first on my own. Kasia was still very groggy and barely aware of her surroundings and our son was undergoing complex tests in intensive care. The doctors had said that it was touch and go for him and the next twenty-four hours were critical.

"Let's give him a name now, just in case. We cannot call him Patricia, how about Patryk?" She said with tears welling up in her eyes.

"Fine, Patryk it is." I was so choked up I couldn't say anything else and I sat carefully on the edge of the bed and kissed my wife's forehead. After a few more minutes I managed to compose myself.

"Right I'll go and get the rest of them." I left the ward and headed back to the waiting room.

Patryk made it through the next twenty-four hours and after a few days, Kasia started breast-feeding him. Her tits were absolutely enormous and she was producing enough milk for an army of babies. Patryk suckled well and soon started to put on weight and grow. He had been born with severe scoliosis, curvature of the spine, and his right hand consisted of three *claw* like fingers, but early tests showed that there had been no brain damage. A week later Kasia and Patryk were allowed home.

With nothing more I could do at this point, I went back to work and continued my search for import options.

Polish girls loved dressing up and Michael contacted the costume jewellery company, Cabouchon. This was a network marketing company that sold its jewellery through a group of self-employed agents. It was very popular in the UK in the late 80s and early 90s. The jewellery was attractive, mostly well-made and cheap, so I got hold of some brochures. The Poles thought that this was going to be a winner but there was a big problem. Cabouchon would not let us just buy the jewellery and then sell it in Poland for whatever amount we liked. I explained that my boss would buy US$5,000 worth of their jewellery per month but they were not interested as it contravened the very rules of pyramid selling. Sadly, the whole idea died, as they were not prepared to bend the rules.

I was beginning to run out of ideas and, one or two members of staff, although they liked me and appreciated what I had done for the Group as a whole, wondered what I was still doing there. Grzegorz still supported me despite the fact that, so far, I had spent a lot of time on the phone to Michael Porter, my UK contact, and come up with zilch. One day Michael came up with a stupendous plan.

The Spice Girls were very popular in the UK and so were alcopops. The most popular alcopop was Hooper's Hooch, a vodka based lemon drink launched by the Bass Brewery in June 1995. It quickly became the fashionable 'ladettes' tipple of the time and was widely recognised as the successor to Babycham. It was also heavily criticised for promoting underage drinking so all the anti-alcohol organisations tried to have it banned.

Michael wrote a letter to Bass telling them that he knew of an organisation in Poland that were ideally positioned to distribute Hooper's Hooch there, and if successful, would be the perfect springboard to develop the sale of this exciting new alcoholic beverage in other former Eastern Bloc countries. He got an immediate reply asking for a detailed business plan. He then wrote back to them advising that there was no way in the world was his contact going to divulge any such information and, if they were serious about expanding the alcopop market into the potentially very lucrative Eastern Bloc market, then they better just go and look. He had another quick response saying they would like to send one of the directors of Bass Beers Worldwide Ltd. to visit me in Poland.

My father's health had improved slightly so my parents decided to drive to Poland to see their new grandson. Their itinerary would bring them first to see friends in France then to Bavaria. They would then motor to Prague where they would stay with Marian Sjveda and finally they would drive to Poznan via Krakow.

I was sitting at my desk waiting for them to arrive when Grzegorz's secretary, Agnieszka came rushing in.

"Rupi, Rupi. Mama. Telefon!"

I picked up the receiver that was lying on Agnieszka's desk.

"Hello?"

"Rupert. Oh Rupert! I think your father has just died."

"Mother where are you?"

"I am at a place called the Green Hotel. I was driving and Daddy just suddenly clutched his chest, said that he could not see anything and collapsed. I stopped at this place and the hotel has called an ambulance but I'm sure he has gone."

"I'll be there in ten minutes." No sooner had I put the phone down than it rang again, so I instinctively picked it up.

"Hello can I please speak to Rupert Miller?"

"Speaking."

"Ah! hello Mr. Miller. My name is George Smith from Bass Beers Worldwide Ltd. and I have just arrived in Poland and am staying at Hotel Poznan. I……."

"Look George. I am very sorry to cut you off, but my father has just died in his car and I've got to go and rescue my mother. I'll contact you later at the hotel. Okay?"

"Of course; I'm very sorry. Goodbye."

Grzegorz was in the factory and he, Jacek and I jumped into his car and sped off to the Green Hotel. When we got there the paramedics had already pronounced 'Big Dave' dead. He was lying in the front passenger seat of their Peugeot 406. He was a large man six foot two in height and weighed twenty stone. He had had heart trouble for some time so this was not totally unexpected.

It was Friday lunchtime so we had to move fast. Dying in Poland creates a lot of paperwork, especially if you are a foreigner. The first thing we did was empty his pockets and then the paramedics put him in a body bag and took him off in the ambulance to the local morgue.

My mother was very calm indeed and thank god she was the one behind the wheel. Grzegorz took my mother back to the office and I drove her car back. When we got there Grzegorz sent Piotr Pudliszewski to fetch Kasia and drop Patryk off at Wuthering Heights.

Grzegorz explained that he, Ela and I were going to get all the necessary paperwork done before the end of the day. He suggested that my mother went back to our flat with Kasia and just relax as much as she could. He then offered to take us all out for dinner in the evening.

We transferred the luggage from my parents' car to Piotr's and then the three of them left for my apartment. We found a dozen of bottles of German wine in the boot of my parent's car and Grzegorz commandeered them to use as 'sweeteners' for the numerous officials we were going to come across during the rest of Friday afternoon.

Grzegorz, Jacek and Ela were wonderful and by 6:00pm everything had been fixed. We had a death certificate, we had flights arranged and my father had been put in a lead coffin and was ready to be shipped back to the UK. Needless to say, all the bottles of wine had gone, plus a few bottles of vodka that we had picked up on our travels. We got back to the office and I suddenly remembered George from Bass, so I rang Hotel Poznan. I agreed to meet him the next day at noon.

My mother decided to stay at Wuthering Heights that night with Kasia and her mother. My father had got within five miles of meeting his new grandson so my mother spent the next morning telling little Patryk all about his English grandfather. At noon I went to Hotel Poznan to meet George Smith, the Hooper's Hooch man. We took a taxi to Plewiska where Grzegorz, Ela and Jacek were waiting for us. George then spent the next two hours telling us all about Hooper's Hooch. He explained how it was the latest new drink for the young and how the success showed in the sales figures – 300% growth in the last twelve months in the UK. We thought that this was a fantastic product and just what the Polish market had been crying out for. We tried the samples George had brought with him and then proceeded to demonstrate that we had the capability to be the Hooch distributor in Poland. I told him that I would put together a detailed business plan and send it to him in a week so he could present it to the Bass Board for final approval.

My mother flew back with my father's coffin on Monday afternoon and I drove her car back later in the week. The funeral was on the Friday and my father was buried next to Julian. Loads of people turned up and we had the wake at the same Country House Hotel, Tyddyn Llan as Julian's. 'Two Helpings' Canon Jones officiated and, just like at my brother's funeral, scoffed and drank everything he could lay his podgy holy hands on. I stayed the rest of the weekend with my mother and on Monday I flew back to Poznan to crack on with the business of distributing Hooper's Hooch.

Even with the luxury tax, all the figures stacked up and, subject to the final go ahead, we pencilled in a Hooper's Hooch launch at Christmas. Apart from the Hooch itself there was plenty of very colourful promotional material available, ranging from bunting to large inflatable lemons with wicked faces. Before George left he said he would send over a few cases so we could start testing the market. Ten days later, having got my plan, we were given the exclusive rights to distribute Hooper's Hooch in Poland for a period of six months. We were going to make a great deal of money.

To help me, Grzegorz hired Beata. Beata was a brilliant international swimmer winning a scholarship to an American University where she had learned English. The first thing was to go to all the bars, clubs, restaurants and supermarkets with samples and prices and get their reaction. Virtually all of them said they would order it so Grzegorz decided that Mex would buy two pallets of Hooch, 5,760 bottles in total.

Grzegorz had been importing goods from abroad for nearly seven years and had got to know the freight forwarders and customs officials very well. The freight forwarder that he had always used was the German company, Kuehne and Nagel who had a depot about three miles away. His assigned customs officer was Tomek, a total alcoholic. He had a basic salary of 6 million old zloty per month but cruised around in a brand new white, seven series BMW. Grzegorz reckoned that his actual monthly income, including unofficial emoluments, was close to 45 million zloty. Apart from the cash, several cases of vodka were frequently loaded into the boot of his car.

To start with there was going to be no credit from Bass Beers Worldwide Ltd. The figures involved were small so this did not present any problem but, before we made any payment, we checked and double checked to see if there was anything else the customs required us to do. They came back with an unequivocal 'no'. Just import the booze and pay the duty and tax. We had got the green light. Ela sent the money to Bass Beers Worldwide Ltd and they sent us the Hooch. When it got to Poland it was held up at the border and the customs officers would not release it. Beata got on the phone.

"Well, we have looked at your import and have noticed it is alcohol. Any alcoholic beverage must have labels that are written in Polish, describing the precise contents of the product. The labels on these bottles are all in English and we cannot allow them in. For a fee we can store them for you."

Grzegorz got onto Tomek immediately and after a heated conversation it was arranged that we could send our own truck to the border to pick up the two pallets of Hooch. God knows what this cost Grzegorz, but two days later our Hooch arrived in Plewiska. At the same time we had a letter from the Minister of Agriculture, Food and Fisheries confirming that if we wanted to sell the Hooch it had to have Polish labels. Grzegorz was convinced we were just being pissed about, after all Johnny Walker labels were all in English. He confronted the authorities who explained that the requirement for labels was needed for certain imported alcoholic beverages but not for others. *What a pile of crap!* was our initial reaction, but if they wanted labels then they could have them.

As we were in the paper and printing business, it took no time to get some self adhesive, information bearing labels. All we had to do was to stick a label on each of the 5,760 bottles that were now sitting in one of our warehouses. As I had nothing else to do I took this task on myself. Nobody seemed keen to help me and there were whispers going round the office that this was going to be another one of 'Golden Boy's' madcap ideas that was doomed to failure. Undeterred and, with the continuing support of Grzegorz, I stuck these labels on every bottle. We reported back to the Ministry to get the go ahead to start supplying our increasingly impatient customers. They did not reply. A week went by and they finally sent us a letter asking us for a total breakdown of all the ingredients used in the making of Hooper's Hooch.

Grzegorz went ballistic and demanded a meeting with the Minister. He drove into Poznan City centre and spent two hours fighting with this bureaucratic dickhead. He explained that he had been meticulous in finding out about all the importing rules for such a product and had been told and had it confirmed in writing that nothing, apart from paying the tax and duty, was required, so why all this bullshit now? The Minister was unimpressed and told Grzegorz that if, and when, he complied then he was free to distribute Hooper's Hooch in Poland.

I sent a long fax to Bass Beers Worldwide Ltd. to explain our predicament but also added that we were fully committed and would resolve the problem in time for the Christmas launch. I got a fax back detailing the ingredients of Hooch but also expressing their concerns that maybe we had bitten off more than we could chew. Beata hand-delivered the information to the Ministry and sat for two hours waiting for a response. Finally we had a bit of luck. Beata was given a letter approving the sale of Hooper's Hooch in Poland.

The most popular pub in Poznan was the Dubliner. It was run by Irish nationals and we had selected it for the Hooper's Hooch official launch. Prior to the launch we also delivered Hooch to many other bars and nightclubs. All of them ordered a few cases and we supplied whatever promotional material they wanted. Hooch did not sell. Nobody was interested and the pubs and clubs just could not understand why. Yes, a few bottles were sold, but eventually they just had to give it away. Maybe it did require a big launch? So we continued with our plan to launch at the Dubliner. Advertisements were placed in GLOS WIELKOPOLSKI, the main Poznan newspaper and on the local radio station. On the day of the launch we had students, dressed as lemons, handing out fliers all over Poznan. This proved to be very successful as when we got to the Dubliner there was a queue round the block. More girls, also dressed as lemons, were outside giving customers free samples. The whole place was buzzing.

In the entire evening The Dubliner sold less than forty

bottles of Hooper's Hooch. Grzegorz was not a quitter and was quite accustomed to set-backs so he suggested that we all adjourn for Christmas and reconvene in the New Year.

When we got back from the Christmas break there was another letter from the Ministry. Hooper's Hooch contained a substance called gum arabic. Gum arabic reduces the surface tension of liquids which leads to increased fizzing in carbonated beverages. The letter went on to say that they had read that drinks that contained gum arabic could cause cancer. Therefore, would we please withdraw from any further distribution of Hooper's Hooch. Years later I found out the Ministry had been 'persuaded' by the breweries to scotch the Hooch plan. We never stood a chance.

So far the Hooper's Hooch episode had cost Grzegorz close to US$10,000 and everyone in the company was calling for my head. He called me to his office and we sat facing each other.

"I'm afraid this is the end of the road my old friend."

I knew that this would happen one day and, when I got back to the flat and told Kasia, she was not the least bit surprised.

"It was never going to last forever. What shall we do now?" she asked.

Chapter Fourteen

The next morning I went to the post office, bought some telephone tokens and walked around Sobieskiego until I found a public phone that actually worked. I rang my mother. She was not surprised at the situation with Komax I.

"They got what they wanted out of you and the moment you slipped up you were out. They were very kind dealing with me and your father's death, but it suited them as they still needed you, or thought they did. Okay, you screwed up. What are you planning on doing now?"

"I have no idea. Maybe we will come and see you for a bit if that is okay?"

"Fortune Stanley is staying with me at the moment. I'll have a chat with her and see what we can come up with. Call me in one hour."

I called my mother exactly one hour later. Fortune Stanley was a very rich old friend of my parents and, as the majority of my father's pension had died with him, Fortune kindly offered to sponsor our return to Wales.

Patryk was now six months old and he had been to see a specialist in Poland who had diagnosed severe scoliosis and confirmed that operations may be necessary. My mother had done some research in the UK and told me that she found a specialist hospital near Oswestry in Shropshire. We now had an opportunity to have our little boy checked out in England.

I was not against the Polish medical system, in fact, many of their staff had been trained at the teaching hospitals in Liverpool, but they were badly underfunded and had little modern equipment. Kasia's younger sister, Ewa, wanted to come with us and Fortune's gift just about stretched to cover the extra flight. My mother met us at Heathrow and, as she was going to stay with some friends in London for a few days, gave us her car and got on the shuttle train into town. We drove back to North Wales.

The next day we went to see our GP in Bala, Tecwyn Jones, and got everyone registered. Patryk was referred to see a specialist at the Robert Jones & Agnes Hunt Orthopaedic & District Hospital NHS Trust in Gobowen near Oswestry in Shropshire.

Agnes Hunt was born in Shropshire in 1867 and by the time she was nine, she had developed hip problems. She later became a nurse and in 1900 she founded a convalescent home for children in Baschurch. In 1903, due to her increasing hip problems, she consulted the eminent orthopaedic surgeon Robert Jones in Liverpool. He was so impressed with her and her work, he became the consultant in Baschurch and they started to treat patients of all ages. Today this hospital has the reputation of being the finest orthopaedic centre in the world. We made an early appointment and Patryk was going to be seen by Professor Stephen Eisenstein, the back specialist and Mr. Roberts, the hand surgeon.

Prior to meeting the consultants Patryk required some extensive X-rays. The hand man said he was too small to do anything at this stage and, in any case, he did not believe that major hand surgery would improve dexterity. Eisenstein confirmed that Patryk had severe congenital scoliosis and something would have to be done. He was far too small for an operation and would be for quite a few years, but they did make him a special jacket to try and stop the curvature getting worse. We had now embarked on Patryk's long-term treatment plan and were to continue visiting the wonderful Professor Eisenstein.

My priority was to get a job, any job. I went to the Centre in Llangollen to look for work and sign on. I also put together my rather odd Curriculum Vitae and answered loads of advertisements in the national and local press. When I did get a reply it was only to thank me for my interest but, 'other candidates seem to be more appropriate for the position and I would like to wish you all the luck in the future'.

I could not go back into the world of financial advising because, since I had left, the whole industry had been shaken up and everybody now had to be fully qualified. No more commission inspired long lunches. Well, not for me anyway.

I answered one advert from a company based in Lytham St Annes near Blackpool. They made Doctors' practice booklets for distribution to all patients at the surgeries. The booklets held all the necessary information about the doctors and the practice but also had pages of adverts placed by local businesses. The job on offer was to sell this advertising space. I went to see them as they were the only company that had given me an interview. It was commission only but they would give you an advance to help you get started. There was a two week in-house training course and accommodation and meals were provided. I discussed it with Kasia and as we had nothing to lose I accepted their offer.

There were ten of us on this training course and the first thing I noticed was that everyone was about the same age, early forties, and male. We were a bunch of misfits who had all tried to do various wacky things but had not, for whatever reason, quite made the grade. The course was excellent and I really learned the mechanics of selling. The problem arose when it came to the part of the training which concentrated on how to find the right person to advertise in the booklets.

Naïvely, I thought everyone would want to advertise in a Doctor's practice booklet. Everybody had a booklet and if you were the only optician advertising in it then you would be guaranteed business. Wrong. What I had failed to realise and had not been told was that someone selling advertising space over the telephone was viewed as being even lower than the double glazing salesman. To get customers we had to learn a script, pick up the Yellow Pages and hit the phones. While I was pretty good when I got in front of customers I just could not cold call. I did try to make a few phone calls but after I had been told to 'piss off' by eight out of the first nine calls I made, I packed up and went home.

Ewa had managed to get herself a job as a live-in nanny in Cheshire so Kasia, who did not drive, had been stuck with my mother while I was on this training course. When I got back she was pretty frustrated and really wanted to move. David Rae came over to see us and he lent me some money so I could buy a second hand car. I bought an old Datsun 'Sunny'. What possessed Nissan to call this car 'Sunny' is quite beyond me.

Then, out of the blue, I had a phone call from a charity in Liverpool who was looking for a professional fundraiser. My name had been put forward by an old school acquaintance who was working in Liverpool. He had heard I was about and desperate for work. I went for an interview and was offered the position. It was only £18,000 a year but it was a start. I drove back to Wales in my little car and we had a minor celebration. The next morning I woke up feeling very good and we got on the phone to arrange some cheap accommodation in Liverpool. That evening I had a call from the charity saying that they were withdrawing their job offer as they had found someone else. I was absolutely shell-shocked. Why? They refused to discuss it and said that the matter was now closed. I suspected that they might have called my *favourite* boss from my days in Manchester.

David Rae came to the rescue again. He had a mate who ran a company in North Wales. If you go to any amusement park, theme park or holiday camp, such as Butlins, you will always find stalls where you can win prizes. Pay a pound for three hoops, throw one over the goldfish bowl and you win a large cuddly toy. This company ran these shows and they were always looking for good people to manage a site, like Thorpe Park. The individuals who hosted the shows were usually local students who had to be trained and watched as there was always lots of cash floating about. The management position at Alton Towers was becoming vacant as from the first of September 1997 but until then they wanted me to go and learn the ropes at Thorpe Park.

The amount of people who just threw money away on games that were deliberately designed to look easy but were almost impossible to win on was truly staggering. People did not just give their kids a pound; they gave them a bag full of pounds. The Arabs were the most profligate. They used to give their kids bundles of fifty-pound notes and would spend thousands trying to win a three foot high badly made 'Tweetie Pie'.

One morning I went to work but the whole place was closed. There were a few security guards milling around the external changing rooms so I asked them what was going on.

"Haven't you heard? Princess Diana was killed in a car crash last night in Paris and, as a mark of respect, the Park will be close until Monday."

Bugger me. Diana dead. I could not believe it and went straight back to the pub we were staying in. Kasia was having breakfast and everyone was glued to the telly.

The next morning it was time to get ready to leave for my new posting at Alton Towers. We were about to get into the car when one of the bosses from Llandudno pitched up.

"Ah Rupert, thank god I've caught you. There has been a change of plan. The guy who was due to leave Alton Towers now wants to stay. We don't have anything for you at the moment. You can carry on working the games but I'm afraid you'll have to pay for your own accommodation. Terribly sorry old chap."

I was beginning to get a bit depressed and I am sure that Kasia was getting pretty sick of me. I was supposed to be the hunter-gatherer, not some useless twit who was either in a dead end, low paid job or on benefits. The cost of the accommodation ruled out continuing at Thorpe Park so we returned to Wales. I carried on scouring the newspapers and very soon Christmas was upon us once more. That year it was a drab affair and best forgotten. I was really hoping that 1998 would bring better luck. One Sunday, after lunch, I was thumbing through the job section in the financial part of the *Mail on Sunday* when I saw this advert.

> *Wanted. Experienced Financial Advisors to advise expatriates in Eastern Europe. No qualifications required. Massive tax free income. Must be solvent.*

Well, I was not solvent but I thought why not try. It cannot be any worse than sitting on your bum in a farmhouse in the middle of North Wales. I showed the advert to Kasia and she lit up like a Belisha beacon; an opportunity to go home.

On Monday I rang the number and had a long chat with this very spivvy sounding gentleman. I explained what I had done, that I knew Poland very well and had a Polish wife.

"You sound like just the person I am looking for. You better come and see me." We were very short of money and I did not trust our car to get me to London and back.

It was starting to make those, 'I'm about to die' noises so I persuaded the job centre in Llangollen to pay for my return train ticket.

The Spiv lived in a large house in Belgravia. Everything in his house was either gold plated or turquoise and he was equally revolting. He was in the process of setting up a company in Warsaw which would provide financial advice to expatriates living and working in Poland. These 'expats', as they were commonly known, could be from anywhere, but the most prevalent were the British and Americans. The reality of the situation was that anyone who worked for this company would do so, on a self-employed, commission only basis. That is why the advert stipulated solvency. One had to be able to stand on one's own feet for at least three months. The financial advice was selling monthly savings plans over fifteen to twenty-five years. These plans were issued by the offshore divisions of major UK Life Assurance companies. The proceeds were all tax-free and the performance of the underlying investment funds boasted some fantastic returns. The commissions were enormous and front-end loaded. Regulation was non-existent.

Most of these expatriates were earning very good money and not spending it, so it was not uncommon to find one who had a couple of thousand dollars of surplus income every month. What was he going to do with it? Give it to me! The problem was there were lots of salesmen, just like me, hoping to make a killing off the back of some overpaid American construction engineer or cosmetic whiz-kid.

I managed to persuade Mr. Spiv that, with my experience as a financial advisor and with my knowledge of Poland in general, I could really help him drive the business forward. I also mentioned that I had very influential connections in Vilnius, Riga, Kiev and Moscow. When he heard about the millions of Saddam Hussein dollars waiting to be siphoned out of Eastern Europe, his greedy little eyes lit up and he agreed to fund our flights to Warsaw, pay me a salary of US$3,000 per month and put US$1,000 per month aside for our accommodation for six months.

When we got to Warsaw, Kasia and Patryk caught a train to Poznan. I was going to sort out the flat first and then they would join me. I went to the Sheraton Hotel where the company had just set up an office in the Regus Business Centre. There I met Charles, the office manager with whom I would be staying with until I found a flat. He introduced me to other members of the sales force and took me aside.

"Look, Rupert. Whatever you do, do not tell the others the package you have negotiated with Mr. Spiv, okay?"

"Fine, Charles. No problem."

That evening we all went to the 'Some Place Else' bar and restaurant on the ground floor of the Sheraton and the next morning we got straight onto the estate agents. By mid-afternoon we had a lovely large one bedroom apartment just off Nowy Swiat in central Warsaw. Nowy Swiat is the Bond Street of Warsaw and our flat was very much in the equivalent district of Kensington and Chelsea. Kasia moved down to Warsaw with Patryk, we enrolled him into a nursery school and she quickly got a job as a PA to a senior partner at Ernst and Young.

I had far more experience of selling financial products than any of the others in the office, but that did not really matter as it was bloody difficult to make appointments. The people that we were targeting were either far too busy to see us or one of our competitors had beaten us to it. At that time there were five of six similar firms all chasing after the same goose. Even if you did manage to make an appointment most of them cancelled. The best way was to ask for referrals but, in order to get one, you first had to secure a deal. In the first month I only made two appointments: one cancelled and the other one was with the ultra-aggressive Managing Director of Estee Lauder Polska. He was an American and was dead keen to get some of his salary offshore so I signed him up.

The next problem was payment. On this deal the commission due to me was US$2,250. The Offshore Life Company would pay the commission to Mr. Spiv once they had all the paperwork. This could easily take a week, as post from Warsaw to The Isle of Man was notoriously slow. Mr. Spiv would sit on it for a month in case the deal cancelled. He would then transfer the money to the bank in Warsaw and then Charles would draw it out and pay us. Therefore, it could take up to seven weeks to get paid!

At the end of the first month I was paid my agreed salary and my rent was also paid. During the course of the second month things became more difficult. Getting appointments just became impossible and virtually all the deals that we had done as a whole group cancelled. Fortunately for me, Estee Lauder did not. Everyone was very short of money and quite a few of our team left. I also discovered that we were behind with the office rent. I was not too worried as I had a guaranteed salary and my rent would be paid for another four months. In addition, I had the Estee Lauder commission to look forward to.

One afternoon, just before the end of the month, a very ashen-faced Charles came into the office and told us that there was no money in the bank and he had been desperately trying to get hold of Mr. Spiv. I only had a few hundred dollars left and I had to pay the rent in a few days. I grabbed hold of Charles and asked about my contract and my guarantees.

"Look mate, if there is no money in the bank, your guarantees are not worth the paper they are written on. I was promised that the money would definitely be in the bank today. Let's hope it gets there by tomorrow."

By close of business the following day the cupboard was still bare. Charles had still been unable to talk to Mr. Spiv and, as he usually spoke to him on a daily basis, was now getting very concerned. By the weekend it had become exceedingly clear the rug had been pulled from under the Warsaw operation. When I got back that night Kasia was fuming. The estate agent had been and told us to have the money by Monday morning or we were out. We had no chance of finding any money over the weekend, so on Saturday morning Kasia and Patryk went back to Poznan.

I was in yet another pickle. Entirely my own bloody fault. Just think, if I had not got so wound up by my brother's death I would probably have been working for some financial advisor in London, married to a Camilla, earning £80,000 per annum, had a couple of kids and procured a huge mortgage round my neck. As it was I had lost my wife and child, albeit temporarily, so I hoped. I could not blame Kasia for buggering off as she had probably had enough uncertainty for a lifetime.

At least I still had the flat at my disposal until Monday, there was some food in the fridge and they had not yet cut off the telephone. I decided not to call my mother but I rang my godmother, Mo instead. Mo, or Mona had been Mrs. Sebastian de Ferranti, the one with the butler in Cheshire.

"Hello Mo, it's your errant godson Rupert and I am in a bit of a fix. I am in Warsaw and the company I have been working for has gone under and not met its obligations and I desperately need some money."

"How much do you need?"

"Well, if you could let me have £3,000, that would be fine and I'll pay you back as soon as I can."

"Don't worry about that I'll just deduct it from your inheritance," she joked.

On Sunday I went to Warsaw Zoo and spent ages watching the poor polar bears just pace up and down in their confined space. I then went back to the flat via McDonalds and a supermarket. I had just enough money for a Big Mac, a bar of chocolate and a couple of beers. The next morning I got up early, packed what little I had and left the flat. I certainly did not want to bump into the estate agent and quite frankly, it was not my problem. I had not signed the lease, Charles had.

The Western Union bank was just round the corner and opened at nine so I had to wait a bit. Mo had said she would do it first thing and, as the UK was an hour behind, I assumed that the money would be there. It was, thank god and they gave me £3,000 in crisp £50 notes. I changed some money, rang Kasia and took the first available train to Poznan.

I got back to Wuthering Heights to a rather frosty reception which I had expected. Although it was not my fault that the boss man had not honoured his obligations, it was my total lack of judgement that was in question. My only defence was that I wanted to get back to Poland as soon as I could as I knew Kasia wanted to be there. But, once again I had chosen the wrong vehicle.

While we had been away a telephone had been installed into Wuthering Heights. I asked if I could ring my mother to see if she was okay and to tell her our news. I was given the all clear. She was used to getting bad news from Poland and she reminded me about Patryk's next important meeting with Professor Eisenstein. It was in a week's time. I had not forgotten but did not think it was so soon. One of us would have to go.

"Oh and by the way, Rupert, someone called Anna-May wants you to call." And she gave me a London telephone number. Anna-May? At first I could not place her and then I suddenly remembered that months ago I had sent her my Curriculum Vitae.

She was a financial services headhunter so I rang her immediately. She had some clients that were looking to develop the expatriate market in Poland. They were not bucket shop cowboys, but a very well established South African bank and they would like to see me. Kasia, understandably, was very cautious but agreed that I would take Patryk to England, see Professor Eisenstein and visit this bank in the City.

They were based right in the heart of the City in some very fancy offices. They wanted me to go back to Warsaw and to continue doing what I was doing before but, this time with the backing of a major financial institution, with proper business cards and full administrative support from London. They agreed to pay me a small salary of £750 per month plus commission. All deals would be processed through London and clients would get authenticated correspondence from their head office. Well, this was a proper business and I could see that this had the potential to blow the cowboy brigade out of the fucking water! Without hesitation I accepted.

Patryk's scoliosis hadn't got worse so we flew back to Poznan with this good news and a contract of employment. On this basis Kasia agreed to return to Warsaw. However, this time, we were going to find a cheap flat. Within a couple of days she had found one in Praga district of Warsaw. The flat was small but only £280 per month. We soon found out that this was one of the most dangerous areas of Warsaw but we were used to danger, so what the hell. In any case, lots of families lived there and, as long as nobody found out that I was English, we would not get mugged very often.

To describe that part of Praga, the Bermuda Triangle of Warsaw, as a shithole would be wholly and irresponsibly inaccurate. Many of the old buildings still had bullet holes in them from the Second World War. The place was littered with old style Drink Bars and corner shops selling beer and vodka. Drunks were commonplace, and after dark, gangs roamed the streets looking for easy pickings. Patryk went back to his old nursery just off Nowy Swiat and Kasia got a part-time job in a primary school. The flat did have a telephone and, with the money I still had from Mo, I bought a fax machine, a second hand laptop, a printer and set up my office in our flat. It was August 1998.

I put an advert in the *Warsaw Business Journal* and wrote to lots of potential customers introducing myself and the services that I could now offer. I started to get replies and slowly but surely started writing a bit of business. What really helped was that the company paid my salary and commissions into my new offshore bank account with no delay and, once again, I began to earn some excellent money.

Our neighbours were very poor and were always borrowing money from us. It wasn't large amounts, fifty to a hundred zloty. Mother and father lived in a pokey one bedroom flat, but their daughter, son-in-law and grandson, who was the same age as Patryk, also lived there. They were all unemployed and perennially miserable. One day Kasia was coming back from work and she met our neighbour's daughter on the tram. She was petrified that she was going to get caught without a ticket so Kasia gave her one. When they got back to the block of flats she invited Kasia in for a coffee, but when she knocked on her door there was no reply so she knocked again and shouted.

"Pawel! Pawel!" But still no reply. She thought this was most odd. She knew her parents were out but her husband should be in looking after their son. Suddenly she heard crying coming from inside the flat.

"Maybe he's just popped out for some fags?" Kasia offered.

"No. No, he'd never do that. Something's definitely wrong and I do not have a key. We'll have to break the door in."

There was no way they could do it on their own so they went to look for help. Outside, they found a couple of builders on a tea break, who came to their rescue. They broke in to find the baby crying in his cot and her husband hanging from the pipes in the bathroom. He was wearing an old pair of underpants and a T-shirt and had strung himself up with a belt.

Once the builders saw this they scarpered; so Kasia had to help this wretched woman cut her husband down. He wasn't quite dead so Kasia rushed to our flat and rang for an ambulance. Shortly both the ambulance and police arrived. As soon as they had established that there had been no shenanigans, the police departed and after the paramedics had pronounced him dead, they carted him off. Kasia invited this poor girl and the baby in for a cup of tea. Surprisingly, she didn't appear that upset and told Kasia that the suicide rate in 'The Bermuda Triangle' was the highest in Warsaw.

There was little hope for families like hers. Kasia asked her what she was going to do.

"Well, I'm young, pretty and broke. I have no choice. My parents will look after Pawel, Jnr. and I will work the hotels." The saddest part was that they were now going to be far better off than when her husband was alive.

I used to take Patryk to playschool every morning on my way to meetings with customers, and Kasia would pick him up after she finished at 4:00pm. The year was growing older and the nights were drawing in. Our street in Praga, ul. Rowna was at the end of the tramline and from the stop we had to walk two hundred yards down the street to our block of flats. By the time Kasia had picked up Patryk and made the tram trip to Praga it was nearly dark and the remaining street lights had been trashed. The local council had given up repairing them as they were demolished almost immediately after they were fixed. The last thing a gang of villains wanted was a well-lit street.

One night Kasia got off the tram and started to push Patryk's buggy along the pavement. Two youths suddenly jumped out of a small alleyway, pushed Patryk and his buggy into the road, grabbed Kasia by the throat and, with a huge knife, cut the straps off her hand bag and ran off with it. She thought they were going to stab her. In hysterics, she picked Patryk and the buggy out of the gutter and, with him now screaming his little head off, ran home as fast as she could.

Luckily I was in and she just grabbed hold of me and sobbed. Her make-up was smeared all over her face and she was violently shaking.

"Tomorrow," she stammered, "I am going back to Poznan with Patryk. You can do what you like."

Thankfully, all we had lost was a handbag, a few cosmetics and a bit of cash and by the next morning Kasia was feeling much calmer and realised that it was not practical to just get up and go; so we planned that we would leave in a week. I rang the landlady, Kasia resigned from her job and we took Patryk out of his playschool. It would not hinder my business at all as I could easily operate from Poznan and go to Warsaw for meetings as needed. There were also quite a few expatriates beginning to come to Poznan.

Our decision to move was further endorsed when I was surrounded by six young men early one evening on my way home. In a split second I recalled a story I had heard on *Parkinson* related by the wonderful Jazz man, the late George Melley.

Many years ago he was on the subway in New York wearing his usual colourful attire, when he was approached by a gang of hoodlums with intent to rob him. He stood up and confronted them.

"Before you rob me I would like to recite some of my favourite poetry," and started. Well, the hoodlums thought he must have been some evil wizard with magical powers as they backed away and jumped off the train at the next stop.

"MY NAME IS RUPERT BEAR!" I screamed at these hoodies. "IF YOU THINK YOU ARE GOING TO MUG ME YOU ARE VERY MUCH MISTAKEN. BE OFF WITH YOU, YOU BEGGARS!" I then started singing 'God Save the Queen' at the top of my voice. It had exactly the same effect. They stared at me, blinked with incredulity and ran off into the night.

Now back in Poznan Kasia decided to finish her university degree, but in English. I continued plying my trade both in Warsaw and Poznan. I picked up more American clients and also started setting up offshore companies and bank accounts for small businesses who wanted to *reduce* their tax liabilities. But as bad luck would have it, two things happened that changed everything.

If you were an American, the IRS (Internal Revenue Service) stipulated that you had to declare your worldwide income and assets irrespective of where you lived. The IRS had heard about some of these British run, offshore investment plans, companies and bank accounts that were being sold, and made it publicly known that they were going to investigate. The Americans accounted for about seventy percent of the expatriate community then and had far more disposable income.

Several of these offshore companies suddenly stopped accepting American applications. One even contacted all of its American investors, including my clients, saying that they would no longer be associated with a US citizen and they would be returning their money. Obviously it was not wise to mess with the IRS. Soon all companies were steering clear of the Yanks.

I need not have worried too much about losing my clients because the second thing that happened was fatal. One of the very big cheeses in London found out that the bank had one, totally unqualified representative in Warsaw, over whom they had little, or no control. That was me and I was asked to cease trading immediately.

Now I was in the biggest pickle of them all; little money left and none due in. I have been through this all before but what was I going to tell Kasia this time? Well, for a couple of weeks - nothing. I continued going to Warsaw pretending to do business but there was no business to be had. I started coming home late and a little the worse for wear. I had a predilection for alcohol and this strengthened when problems arose. When she looked at my laptop and found that I had had no emails from London for two weeks, it became very difficult to hide.

This time the family and Kasia said that 'enough was enough'. My performance was not acceptable. I had virtually no money and what cash I did have was being spent on booze. It was obvious I had no financial future in Poland so they put me on a bus back to the UK and told me to sort myself out permanently. Kasia thought that she would never see me again. It was now the new Millennium, January 2000 and I had lost everything.

Chapter Fifteen

Before I left Poznan I had just about had enough time to ring my mother and ask if I could stay for a few days. Reluctantly she agreed, but to be fair I had not given her any option. After a thirty hour bus journey, I arrived in Llangollen in North Wales where my mother was waiting for me. She wasn't pleased to see me and, for the half an hour it took to get back to her house, we did not exchange a single word. When we got back, she was the one to break the ice.

"Hungry?"

"Yes, but can I make a telephone call please?

"Kasia?"

"Yes."

"Are you sure that's wise?"

"Look, I know I have messed up in a big way but I am not just going to roll over. I'm going to get my family back and I'm going to start now." I rang Kasia, told her I was at my mother's and said that I loved her.

"Whatever." she whispered and put the phone down. It was a start, a rather inauspicious start, but a start nevertheless. I made myself some baked beans on toast, a cup of tea and went to bed. I lay awake for a few hours planning my comeback. The first thing to do was to quit the booze and the fags. Apart from anything else I had no money for them. I was not going to go on the dole and I made it my aim to get a job, any job within one week. With my plan established I fell asleep.

The next morning I woke up very early and, as it was Thursday, I borrowed my mother's car and went to the local village and got all the newspapers. Thursday was job offer day in many newspapers. I got back and took my mother a cup of coffee in bed. She was quite surprised and thanked me.

"What are you going to do today?" she asked.

"I'm going to get a job. I've been to the village and got all the papers and now I'm going to start sifting through all the offers."

My brother, who now lived in the converted barn next to my mother's house, let me use his computer. I wrote a new Curriculum Vitae and printed off half a dozen copies. I decided to embellish it because if I had written down the truth no one would have even given me an interview, let alone a job. As it was, it was going to be highly unlikely I'd get any employment other than, maybe as a storeman in a farmer's market. However, I plodded on through the papers and then I saw an advert that caught my eye.

> *Wanted for North Wales. Salespeople. No experience required as full training given. OTE £50,000 for the right candidates. Call Ken on 0800 677677 for an immediate interview.*

I thought, well I'm a salesman and I'm in North Wales, I think I'll investigate further. A girl answered and told me that she'd get Ken to call me back soon. Half an hour later he rang.

"Hello. Rupert Miller?"

"Yes."

"Can you come to the Beaufort Hotel just outside Mold for a chat, say at 2:00pm today?"

"Look what's this job all about?"

"I have not got the time to explain everything now. Can you or can't you?"

"Okay, I'll be there." Puzzled, I put the phone down. Mold was only twenty minutes' away so I went back upstairs to ask my mother if I could borrow her car.

"Why do you want the car this afternoon?" she asked in a rather mistrusting manner.

"I have a job interview in Mold." And I showed her the advert.

"Looks like a bit of a con to me."

"Well if I do not go then I will not find out, so can I have the car please?"

"Well, all right, if you have to."

I spent the rest of the morning combing through the papers but found nothing else. Fortunately, since our escape from Lithuania, I had put on a bit of weight so my old suits fitted me quite well. I selected the best one, gave it a sponge and a press and, after an early lunch, set off to Mold.

Ken was a short scruffy looking bloke and, although he was wearing a tie, his top button was undone. This caused a bit of alarm as after my dealings with Mr. Spiv, I wasn't keen on dealing with anyone 'unprofessional' again. Putting that thought aside, Ken ushered me into a room and offered me a seat.

"Can you walk?" he asked.

"Yes I can."

"Good. Can you talk?"

"Of course I can." I replied, eagerly anticipating his next bloody daft question.

"Right, you're hired. The training course starts here tomorrow 9:00am. Any questions?"

"Yes, lots. For a start, why have you not even asked to see my CV?

"Look, over the next three days I'm going to teach you how to sell adjustable beds. After that, the company will give you between two and three pre-set appointments every day from Monday to Saturday inclusive. You look the part and if you learn how to do it, I cannot see you having any problems earning £35,000 in your first year. It is commission only and hard work but you'll be your own boss. If it doesn't work, you'll leave, but if you don't try you will never know, will you? Just you coming here today is evidence enough to me that you're desperate."

I inwardly sighed. He was absolutely right. I had no option but to give it a try, so I agreed to turn up for training the next morning. My problem was that I had no car. The Datsun had long since died so I managed to borrow an old banger from the owner of the village stores. Although the position was commission only they did have a scheme whereby they would pay you a very small retainer as an advance on future anticipated earnings to help you get started. I told my mother, who seemed quite pleased, and rang Kasia that evening and so, surprisingly, was she.

The next morning I got there early. Ken was in a small conference room setting up his presentation. There were eight place settings each with a name card and one by one the others started to arrive. One guy was wearing jeans and a T-shirt and had an earring in each ear. Ken took one look at him.

"I thought I told you yesterday that if you wanted to start then lose the jewellery and the order of dress was a smart suit?"

"Yeah... Err…Well mate I ain't fuckin' got one, av' I?"

"Well in that case I suggest you leave right now." At which point our sartorial CEO left the room. One down, seven to go.

By 9:00am we were all sitting round the table and Ken started telling us all about adjustable beds. By lunchtime I was beginning to think that I might just be able to do this. During our lunch break one of the other sardines came up to me.

"Great this, innit?"

"Well I must say that, after an unimpressive start, I am beginning to think that selling adjustable beds might be good."

"Nah mate! Not the friggin' job, the free grub." At which point Ken ushered us towards the hotel buffet, an 'eat as much as you want' type of place. My new friend over loaded his plate with an interesting mixture of food and sat at a table by the window.

Cold salmon and curry was not my idea of a square meal but I was intrigued to find out more about this blatant freeloader so I decided to join him. He was a professional sponger. He would go on as many courses as he could just for the free lunches, coffees, sweets and he would also nick as much as he could from the hotels.

"This is the third time in as many years I've had lunch off this company." He proudly announced, puffing out his bloated gut before returning to the buffet for a second helping. It crossed my mind to spill the beans to Ken but then I thought, well good luck to the bloke. Who was I to spoil his fun?

After lunch we continued until 5:00pm and then went home. The next day we were down to five, which included our 'Galloping Gourmet', of course, and by the end of the second day I really felt that I could earn a living selling adjustable beds. By the morning of the final day we had lost one more sardine and after an enormous lunch our freeloader departed. Only three out of eight lasted the course. Ken told us that on Sunday evening we would get a call from head office with our three appointments for Monday. He wished us the best of luck, got into his car and buggered off. I spent the entire weekend going through the sales blurb I had been given and practicing my presentation. I was also told to buy some nice biscuits.

I got my three appointments on Sunday night. The first one was in Colwyn Bay at 10:00am, the second one was in Rhyl at 2:00pm and the third one was in Denbigh at 6:00pm. So on Monday morning I set off to Colwyn Bay really buoyed up and looking forward to start making some money again.

Our prospective customers were cold-called from lists that had been bought in from various sources. If they agreed to a visit right away they were given the chance to win an adjustable bed. These meetings were supposed to be with individuals who had medical problems such as arthritis and for whom an adjustable bed would be ideal. We had been taught a very structured presentation. The first part was to get in the appointed house and that is why we had to take biscuits, a type of bribe. Again I had been very naïve. I thought that everyone would want one of these wonderful products and, indeed everybody did, but nobody wanted to pay for them so, by the time you arrived, many appointees had gone off the whole idea and hidden behind the sofa.

Once you had charmed your way into the house it was then a question of just relaxing them and being very friendly. Then you would show them a video and give them a practical demonstration using pillows, a sample mattress and a hand held electric massager in their bedroom. Once that was over it would be a question of pricing and hopefully getting a payment off them for as much as possible there and then. If you could not get a good price then you could telephone your 'Manager' to try and get a better price for the customer. The higher the price the higher the commission.

My first appointment was with a young, unemployed couple who had three small children. I had no trouble getting in when they saw the free biscuits. I rang my manager to explain there had obviously been a mistake.

"Never pre-judge Rupert. Do a full demonstration. Do not cut any corners. You never know. They might have just won the lottery."

However, they had not, and while they loved the idea of having an adjustable bed they did not have a pot to piss in. My second appointment was not in. The company rule was to wait one hour and then leave. It was now 3:00pm and my next appointment was in Denbigh at 6:00pm. Rhyl to

Denbigh was only twenty minutes' drive so what in the hell was I going to do for the next two hours and forty minutes? I ended up walking around Sainsbury's for an hour and a half and then had a cup of tea in the in-store café. My third appointment would not let me in.

The next day none of my appointments would let me in but on the third day I did manage to do three full presentations but failed to make a sale as I was being too nice. When the customer said 'I want to think about it'. I'd just say, "Okay", and leave, instead of nailing their feet to the floor until they signed the cheque. After the last appointment my manager rang me.

"Look mate you have got to be tougher. This is not a fucking picnic. Everybody loves our beds so by not forcing the sale you are not only letting yourself down but you are also letting down the customer. If you do not sell you will not be able to put food on the table so, as soon as you start to follow the script, then you will start to earn, understand?"

He was right and what he said very much reminded me of what the prostitutes used to say our soldiers in Belize. "No Munni, No Fukki." I had to get tougher and quickly.

The next day I made my first sale which took me back to the good old days in Kaunas. It is a terrific feeling when you make a sale and once you have one under your belt more follow. After a few weeks I began making regular sales and commission cheques started to arrive. Sometimes it was a few hundred pounds and sometimes closer to a thousand. One week I got paid a massive £2,500. My target of £35,000 in my first year was looking increasingly likely!

I gave the 'banger' back to the village stores, bought my mother's Volvo and re-paid David Rae. I also started to speak to my wife more often and sent her money. Patryk was due to see Professor Eisenstein again in July and I was hoping she would come over with him and stay.

I kept my fingers crossed and worked every appointment they gave me. My plan was to get my family over and move from my mother's house to Wrexham as this would be far better for my business, good for Patryk as his hospital would be virtually next door, and Kasia would be living in a town; not stuck in some farmhouse surrounded by sheep.

My plan worked and I sent her enough cash to buy tickets to fly to Manchester Airport. There was a little nervousness to start with but it soon passed and Patryk was very pleased to see his daddy again. His daddy couldn't find a superlative powerful enough to mirror his feelings. We spent one day with my mother and then rented a *Coronation Street* type terraced house in the centre of Wrexham. I spent the summer working while Kasia sorted out our new Welsh nest and started taking driving lessons. Patryk had his appointment with Professor Eisenstein who told us that in a year or two he would need to have some corrective surgery to help stop and possibly reverse the curvature of his spine. I asked him what would happen if he did not have it done.

"In my opinion, if nothing is done, then when he reaches puberty the curvature will accelerate and he'll end up looking like the hunchback of Notre Dame."

"Okay. We understand. How complicated is this going to be?"

The Professor then proceeded to explain what would happen. They would open him up at the front and the back so they could move all his organs to either side to allow them full access to his spine. A notch would then be cut out of each vertebra on one side of his spine. They would then remove a rib and fuse it to the spine in a vertical position, using the notches as support for the rib. The idea would be to slow down the growth on one side of the spine and increase it on the other and hopefully by the time he had stopped growing he should be about 85% straight. We listened intently.

"How dangerous is this operation?" My mind flicked back once more to visions of that half cow in the meat market in Vilnius, an image now indelibly printed on my memory.

"Well, any major back surgery can be potentially dangerous but not life threatening. However, as we have never tried this operation before, we do not know." One thing we liked about Eisenstein was his candour.

Patryk had to wear his little hard plastic jacket 24/7 and only took it off at bath time. It was horribly uncomfortable for him, and used to often pinch him under his armpits, but we bit our lips in the hope that we were going down the right track. Was it the radiation from Chernobyl that was responsible or one or both of us? My mother blamed herself for Julian's condition as I'm sure Kasia did for Patryk's. Both were way off the mark. It happened for whatever reason and, as a family, we had to get on and deal with it.

Kasia needed to change her status in the UK. This involved a trip to the Home Office in Croydon with all the necessary documents to prove that she was my wife and that I could support her and she was not here just to try and get benefits. After queuing for four hours outside the Home Office building, we then handed in our papers, took a numbered ticket and sat in the waiting room. Three hours later our number came up and after a five minute interview she had '*leave to remain in the United Kingdom but no recourse to public funds*'.

In no time at all Kasia got a part-time job working for a small family business that made prescription lenses and Patryk started at St Mary's Catholic primary school in Wrexham. I continued selling adjustable beds.

One day I not only nearly lost my job but also my life. It was a gloriously warm September evening and I had a 6:00pm appointment in the Wirral. I arrived at a very grand house in the smartest district. There was a huge fat Mercedes parked outside so I thought that I could do a big deal here. I rang the doorbell and after a few minutes a stunningly beautiful six foot, bikini-clad girl opened the door.

"Is Mr. Blake in please?" I stammered.

"No, but I'm Mrs. Blake can I help?"

"I'm from the adjustable bed company and I........."

"Oh good," she interrupted, "do come in. It's me that made the enquiry. My husband is not interested."

"Well I do need to really talk to both of you. Will your husband be home soon?"

"Look, my husband works very late and he never comes back until at least 10:00pm every night. Furthermore, it is me that wants the bed, and if I like what you have to show me then it will be me buying it, not my husband so let's get on okay?"

This was a definite deal and so I started my presentation by showing her the video after which I rather nervously asked her to show me her bedroom.

"Follow me." She beckoned and started walking very slowly up the stairs. I followed with my mattress sample and my electric hand held massager. When we got into the bedroom she sat on the corner of the bed, looked up at me with her big, hazel puppy dog eyes and said.

"What do you want me to do now?"

This was making me very nervous and I started piling pillows and cushions at the headboard end of the bed.

"Right can you please just lie back on the bed?" I asked and she did. I then put the sample mini mattress under her legs, plugged in the massager, turned it on and put it under the pile of pillows supporting her back.

"How does that feel, Mrs. Blake?" I said desperately trying not to appear to be ogling her perfect body.

"Wonderful and my name is Miranda, not Mrs. Blake. Why don't you join me?" and with that she sat up and took off her bikini top to reveal a pair of juicy breasts. At that very moment I heard the front door open.

"I'm home darling. Where are you?"

"I'm upstairs in the bedroom with a strange man." She answered and made no effort to cover herself up whatsoever. She just lay there smiling at me. I thought that it was most definitely the time to leave so I unplugged the massager and grabbed the mini mattress by which time this man who was, almost certainly her husband, had arrived in the bedroom to find his wife lying on the bed half naked and me standing next to her holding the massager which looked like a rather large vibrator.

"What in the fuck is going on here?" he demanded, his eyes darting from me to his wife and back again. "Who are you?"

"Darling, he's the man from the bed company and……"

Before she could finish he took a swing at me with his left fist but missed.

"I'm going fucking kill you. What have you been doing to my wife?"

Instead of answering I made a bolt for the door, ran down the stairs, picked up my briefcase, leapt in to my car and made a hasty getaway. Quite frankly I was very glad he had come home earlier than expected because that lady was extremely dangerous.

Autumn was soon upon us and I carried on selling as many adjustable beds as possible. The problem was that I never got home until ten at night and had to work on Saturdays. To begin with Kasia put up with it, but by Christmas she was getting pretty pissed off and pointed out that she almost saw more of me when she was in Poland. We agreed that after Christmas I would start looking for a new job.

Willowbrook came to the rescue and I started just before Easter 2001 selling their electric mobility scooters. In my first week I made over £3,000. What an excellent career move.

Apart from being self-employed, one of the great joys of the business was that every day was different. One day I met Mr. and Mrs. Thomas who lived in a council house along with their two daughters and sons-in-law. The Thomases were in their early fifties and their daughters and respective husbands, in their mid to late twenties.

All six were so fat that none of them could walk properly. Mrs. Thomas wanted to buy a scooter but was over thirty stone in weight and even our biggest scooter only had a twenty-eight stone capacity. The rest of the family was of similar proportions. They were all very nice and visibly upset that I had been unable to make a sale due to their excessive bulk, so they very kindly invited me to stay for lunch.

In the kitchen there were two gas cookers rigged up to a large gas bottle in the corner. All eight rings were fired up and on each ring there was a large pan full of deep frying chips. On the draining board there were four loaves of white sliced bread and each slice had been liberally coated with margarine. I thanked them for their mouth-watering offer, but declined.

One customer paid for his £3,000 scooter in loose change so I left his house with four Tesco bags full of coins. Some houses were so revolting it was impossible to stay in them without almost dying of asphyxiation. In one I went to there was an old man who had very bad emphysema. He was connected to a vast oxygen cylinder via tubes inserted into his nose. Despite the fact that he could hardly breath, was coughing up blood every five seconds, he was still chain smoking.

In another house I found a twenty-five year old girl with learning difficulties who had lost her legs as a result of a car accident. Her uncle was living with her, as her guardian, because her father was serving time for raping her while she was strapped in the wheelchair. They lived in total squalor in a tiny council flat in Manchester. Cat shit was smeared all over the kitchen floor and, judging by the number of empty pizza boxes littered all over the place, they must have been monophagous. Without the correct training I'd have made my excuses and left. However, despite the darkness and rain, I got this girl onto the scooter and she immediately began to laugh. Seconds later she was zooming around the car park, lights on and continuously pressing the horn. We couldn't get her off and by the time her uncle finally caught her she was drenched to the skin but deliriously happy. The uncle produced six thousand pounds in cash from a cornflake box which he had hidden under the kitchen sink. He bought two scooters, one for him and one for his niece.

One Saturday I went to see George Sidebottom in Knaresborough, North Yorkshire. He wanted to see a power chair. I rang the bell and the door was opened by a huge man with a shaved head which was covered in swastika tattoos. He was sporting a goatee beard, must have been six foot five and about thirty-five years old. In addition to his head, he had more tattoos on his neck, down the full length of his arms and all over the back of his hands. He was wearing tight jeans, bovver boots and a clean white, very tight T-shirt. Each ear was adorned with rings, as were his eyebrows, lips and nose.

He ushered me in without speaking and then sat in the corner of the room. He then just glared at me while I attempted to do a presentation for Mr. Sidebottom who, I assumed, was his father. It was very intimidating and I was half expecting this monster to jump up out of his seat and put me to death. I eventually completed the demonstration and gave Mr. Sidebottom the price.

"What do you think son?" The old man said, turning to face the gorilla in the corner.

"Ooh, Dad I think it's great. Buy it." He replied in a very high pitched, squeaky voice with a broad Yorkshire accent. After I had done the paper work and relieved Mr. Sidebottom of £3,500 in cash, the monster produced a pot of tea and some delicious fairy cakes. It turned out that the object of my terror was a pastry chef in Harrogate.

One day my satellite navigation system took me to the middle of nowhere and the country lane I was on was barely wide enough for my van. I eventually found my destination.

I was greeted by a very old rusty gate and through this gate ran a dirt-track road into a small copse. I opened the gate, drove down the track and after about a mile I came across a very dilapidated farm house. Next to the farmhouse there were a few outbuildings with some pre-war farm machinery lurking inside. I stopped my van in the middle of the farm yard, got out and walked to the front door. There was no bell or knocker so I banged on it with my fist and waited. Several minutes passed but there was still no answer so I waded through the thick undergrowth down the right hand side of the house to see if there was a window I could actually see through. Eventually I found one at the back of the house and peered through it. I saw a rather small Father Christmas sitting, slumped in a wheelchair. I tapped on the window and he immediately woke up, looked at me, smiled and then pointed towards his front door. I made my way back to the front door which he had opened.

Mr. Eric Postlethwaite had no legs and was sat in a prehistoric electric wheelchair which he manoeuvred by fiddling with the joystick, mounted on the right arm of this ancient conveyance. He had shoulder length thick snowy hair and a white bushy beard that stopped at his navel. Apart from the leg department, he was Father Christmas personified.

He ushered me in and I followed him through the kitchen and into the living room where he asked me to sit down on the sofa. Apart from several empty silver foil ready meal containers everything in the kitchen and sitting room was over fifty years old, covered in dust and had not been touched for god knows how long. In the kitchen sink there were some dirty plates and some rusty old knives and forks that had been waiting to be washed up since the early 50s or so it seemed. Next to the sofa there were heaps and heaps of *Reader's Digest* magazines. I picked one up. It was the July 1948 edition.

"I saw your scooter advertisement in the latest edition of *Reader's Digest* and, as I have fallen out with my carer who does my shopping, I thought I better get one of your machines so I can do my own in the future. I do hope you have brought some models to show me?" he suddenly spouted.

"Of course I have, Sir." I replied and after my preliminary assessment we went outside to try the big Ultraglide 8mph mobility scooter. I thought that he would have had trouble getting on it but he was well prepared. He had a shuffle board. This was a piece of wood, eighteen inches wide and three foot long that he used to shuffle from his wheelchair to anything else. Once sat on the scooter I showed him how the controls worked and he took it for a test drive. He drove down the track, out of the gate and disappeared up and over the hill.

After about half an hour I became a bit concerned so I jumped in the van and set off to try and find him. I reached the top of the hill and there, in the distance, I saw him driving the scooter back in my direction, so I waited. When he approached I noticed that the baskets on the machine were full. He'd taken the opportunity to do a spot of retail therapy. On reaching my van he just sailed straight past as though he had not seen me. I had to drive another mile away before I found somewhere wide enough to turn round and when I returned to his house he was already inside.

"How much?" he asked.

"It's £3,500, including the guarantees, insurance, breakdown cover and delivery."

Like all salesmen are taught, I then shut up. He did not say anything for a few minutes and then he asked me to go over to the Welsh dresser and open the bottom right hand cupboard door. Inside there were six Tupperware containers. He told me to take one out and bring it over to him.

"How much… £3,500 was it?" He quizzed.

"Yes. £3,500."

He took the lid off the container and handed it to me. It was full of twenty pound notes neatly folded into £100 parcels and each one secured with a paper clip. He instructed me to take out the correct amount but when I had there was easily enough left in that container to buy another three scooters. There were still five more boxes in the Welsh dresser. He signed all the papers and, although it was none of my business, I thought I better mention that having all that cash around was probably not a good idea and that he should put it in the bank.

"I've got too much in the bank as it is and I like having cash around just in case I want to buy something like today. If anyone tries to rob me I'll just shoot them," and with that he pulled a service revolver from a drawer.

Curiosity got the better of me so I asked how come he had amassed so much money. I expected him to tell me to bugger off but he didn't. He set off in his wheelchair and beckoned me to follow him. We went into a side room where there was a state-of-the-art stockbrokers' dealing desk. He had computers, printers, fax machines, telephones, scanners and all of it was the latest up-to-date equipment. He had the *Financial Times* delivered every day and subscribed to *Bloomberg* magazine.

Eric Postlethwaite had been a rear-gunner in a Lancaster bomber which was shot down in 1943. He was the only survivor but his legs had been riddled with bullets so they were amputated. His parents had been killed in the blitz in London and had left him a pile of cash and the farmhouse in Yorkshire. After he had recovered from his injuries and the War was over he moved into the house in 1946. He had always been keen on the markets so he started playing the stock market and had done so ever since. Before I left I took his shopping into the house and asked him if there were any other chores he'd like me to attend to. He thanked me but said he'd kiss and make up with his carer.

Most of our customers paid for their scooters in cash or by cheque, credit/debit card and some took advantage of our monthly payment plan. There were, however, a few who paid for them by surrendering all or part of the mobility component of their disability living allowance. This allowance is a tax free, non-means tested benefit that can be paid to anyone who is disabled. Once such a customer has selected a scooter the salesman would have to escort the client to their local benefit office to get a special mobility form stamped.

These benefit offices seemed to attract, mainly on Fridays, charming young single mothers pushing prams. The ones I visited in Liverpool provided the most entertainment. On one occasion, a *delightful* young lady with '*I'm Barry's Bitch*' tattooed on the nape of her neck, suddenly kicked-off.

"Look, I went to Iceland a few days ago and stocked up with food for the baby but last night we had a fuckin' power cut and the fuckin' fridge-freezer's knackered.

Everything's ruined and it's fuckin' Friday and I've got no fuckin' money to feed me fuckin' baby and I'm worried fuckin'stiff it's going fuckin' die of fuckin' starvation. I need yer fuckin' 'elp. Can yer give us a fuckin' tenner?"

All said in a very strong Liverpool accent with a fag hanging out of one side of her mouth, despite the no smoking signs and simultaneously swigging lager out of a can of Carlsberg Special Brew. Fully protected by a six inch thick glass screen the answer was nearly always the same. 'No'.

"Look you fuckin' bastard, when the baby's father gets out of fuckin' prison he's gonna fuckin' kill yer."Shortly after her tirade she was escorted from the premises by the Merseyside Police. I did once witness a small emergency payment being made to one of these dysfunctional n'er-do-wells, which was immediately exchanged for alcohol and tobacco in the CO-OP across the road.

Julian had now been dead for more than ten years and it was barely five since my father's fatal heart attack in Poland; yet the Grim Reaper was sharpening his scythe again. We had always joked that my mother would out live all of us as she was never ill. When she was diagnosed with liver cancer in early 2002, nobody could believe it. We thought it was all a very embarrassing mistake so we asked the hospital to double-check. They had not.

The cancer took hold so fast that the doctors told her that there was no point trying to treat it, and anyway my mother had the most fantastic head of hair. The thought of losing it was most definitely not on her agenda. She was incredibly dignified throughout her illness and I could see precisely where Julian's panache and bravery had come from. Her last days were made far more comfortable than they might otherwise have been thanks to the tireless and selfless attention afforded to my mother by Clunie and Silvia. We buried her ashes on top of my father and Julian. Once again we had the wake at Tyddyn Llan, but Canon Jones, our *voracious vicar*, was nowhere to be seen. He must have died of a surfeit of fish pie, cottage pie and house wine.

The Miller family had now lost three members in a very short time so I was extremely nervous when we gave Eisenstein the go-ahead to operate on Patryk. It was the eighth of January 2003. He was six and a half years old and just about big enough to endure this major surgery.

Apart from Eisenstein there were two other surgeons involved; a spinal cord specialist, whose job was to stabilise the spinal cord and Mr. Trivedi, Eisenstein's successor-in-waiting. As this was a 'first', they filmed the whole operation so they could use it for training in the future.

Despite being a success the operation knocked the stuffing out of us. For the first time since he was born we had handed our son over to some virtual strangers to experiment on. Wow. That was scary. 'Never again', we prayed. Patryk took weeks to recover but thank god he could now do without his ghastly restricting jacket and hopefully he would begin to straighten.

Although I had taken a little time off I still managed to qualify, along with a few others, for the Willowbrook annual sales trip. This year it was an accompanied all expenses paid holiday to Las Vegas. I had never been to the States before and neither had Kasia. The party was for four days and we planned to leave Patryk with Kasia's sister, Ewa who had also married an Englishman and was living in Hampstead, North London. We would then drive to Gatwick where we were booked into a hotel. We left Wrexham at tea time and had just passed Toddington services on the M1, when Patryk woke up.

"Daddy, I need a pee."

Why do small children always wake up just after you have passed the services?

A mile further down the motorway I spotted a works entrance on the hard shoulder so I pulled over. We got to Ewa's at about 8:00pm, had a quick cup of coffee and drove to Gatwick. About five miles out of Gatwick we pulled into a service station. I suddenly notice that the blue folder with our tickets and passports was no longer on the backseat. We frantically searched the car but no folder. Kasia rang Ewa in case we had left it there but no joy. It had definitely been put in the car so we deduced that the only place it could be was on the hard shoulder where Patryk had had his pee. It was now 10:00pm.

We turned round and drove back up the M23 and then took the M25 clockwise round London until we hit the M1. We drove up the M1 and got off at the junction just north of Toddington services. We then drove back down the M1 on the inside lane at thirty miles an hour hoping to spot the place where we had stopped. Our task was not made any easier by the thick fog that had suddenly descended upon the motorway and I now could not even see the end of the bonnet, let alone the side of the road. Suddenly the fog lifted for a split second and I saw the works entrance and pulled over. I jumped out and there was our blue folder with passports and tickets inside lying on the hard shoulder.

The next morning we checked in and the first leg of our flight took us as far as Charlotte, USA. We had a four-hour wait and then flew on to Las Vegas. Our accommodation for the duration was to be the MGM Grand, the largest hotel in Vegas with more than five thousand rooms and live lions in a glass cage in the foyer.

It was late and we were all exhausted, so we had a few drinks in the bar and then retired. In our room we had an enormous bed, a beautiful en suite bathroom and the walls were covered in photographs of MGM film stars. We both woke up at 3:00am, raring to go because the jet lag had kicked in. After much tossing and turning, sleep finally got the better of us and the next thing we knew it was 9:00am. We were both famished so, while Kasia was having a bath, I ordered some room service.

"Good morning Mr. Miller, Sir, and how are you this morning, Sir? Oh I can see Mrs. Miller is very well, nice bathroom isn't it? No Sir only joking. We do not have CCTV in the bedrooms or bathrooms. Now Sir, maybe Sir would like to order some breakfast?"

"Yes please we'd like some eggs."

"Certainly, Sir. Fried? Boiled? Scrambled? Poached or coddled?"

"Scrambled please with some sausages and bacon, a pot of fresh coffee and some freshly squeezed orange juice."

"Fine, Sir. Twenty minutes."

The egg thing reminded me of a story a friend of mine told me about the time he was hitch-hiking around America. He got a lift in a juggernaut and the driver stopped for breakfast at a typical truck stop café where he offered to buy my friend breakfast. Like the driver, he ordered steak and was asked by the waitress if he'd like fried eggs with his steak.

"Yes, please."

"How many, five, ten or fifteen?"

Our breakfast was delivered by an immaculately dressed room service attendant who converted the trolley, which was carrying our breakfast, into a dining room table and started to set everything in its rightful place. I had never had such professional room service before. It was wonderful and so was the breakfast.

During the day we were left to our own devices and would meet up with the others for dinner in the evenings. Kasia was well prepared and had already planned the day. We were going to walk the Las Vegas Strip and visit the themed hotels. We visited New York, New York, Excalibur, Caesars Palace, Paris Las Vegas and the Venetian Resort. I went into the Gucci store in the Caesars Palace complex where I noticed that none of the items on display had any prices, so I made a comment to one of the very beautiful and glamorous sales ladies.

"Sir, with all due respect, if Sir needs to know the price then Sir is in the wrong shop."

When they say Las Vegas is open twenty-four hours a day it means twenty-four hours a day and when the hotel staff say 'Have a nice day', although it sounds very cheesy, they actually mean it. It was the most mind-boggling place I had ever seen. It was totally over the top, yet irresistible. Every hotel was enormous and the ground floor of each one was just one vast gambling pit. Roulette and black jack tables mingled with hundreds of one armed bandits. I read somewhere that every time someone walks through the main entrance of the MGM Grand, eighty dollars goes in the till.

When it comes to gambling, I have taken after my maternal grandmother; a flutter, once a year, on a nicely named nag in the Grand National at Aintree. In 1928 my grandmother had a new scullery-maid arriving from Tipperary, Ireland on the day of the big race so she put five pounds to win on a 100-1 outsider called Tipperary Tim. Thick fog cloaked the course that afternoon and caused a massive motorway style pile-up in the last few furlongs of the race. My grandmother's mount was too far behind to be involved so managed to tiptoe through the carnage to finish in first place.

Sadly, I have never had such good fortune and, while my colleagues were losing stacks on the roulette and black jack tables in the casino, I was adhering to the advice given to me by one of the stewardesses on the flight from Charlotte to Las Vegas. The best way to double your money in Vegas is to fold it in half.

Chapter Sixteen

Selling mobility products, although fairly lucrative, only had a certain shelf-life so, for me anyway, Willowbrook was rapidly approaching its sell-by date. Poland had recently joined the European Union and it seemed as though half of the population had come to the UK. The Government had planned for fifteen thousand Poles to arrive in the first year and the same amount in year two. They later admitted that the number of Poles who actually arrived was closer to one million. The unofficial figure is nearer to two. They brought their children with them who needed to be taught English so Kasia, whose Polish teaching qualification now counted, acquired her WQTS (Welsh Qualified Teacher Status) and walked straight into a well-paid teaching job with the Wrexham County Borough Council.

At Sandhurst I had broken my left ankle playing rugby and over the years it has always niggled a bit. Driving a van had made it worse recently so I went to the doctor who diagnosed arthritis and recommended a desk job. I started buying the *Daily Mail* on Thursdays again hoping to find something suitable. Willowbrook were the best company in mobility sales so if I did move it would be into something totally different.

My desire for a change was so acute that I even contacted a few look-a-like agencies to see if they were interested in a dead ringer for Stephen Fry. I was constantly being mistaken for him. A few years ago I came out of a customer's house in Birmingham and was accosted by an anorak.

"I know you, you're Stephen Fry, aren't you?" he grinned inanely, looking impossibly pleased with himself.

"No I am not."

"Oh yes you are," he insisted. "Can I have your autograph?"

"No. My name is Rupert Miller. Here is my business card and that is my van. Do you want to buy a mobility scooter because if you do not piss off immediately you are going to need one?"

"Very clever Mr. Fry. I'm sure this fools the paparazzi but you can't fool old Reginald Bates. Sign here please." And with that he thrust a rather grubby old brown envelope in my general direction. Well, I had never come across such a persistent congenital nincompoop in my entire life. I tried once more to put him off but failed dismally, so I took the envelope, plucked a pen from my inside pocket and asked him.

"Do you spell Stephen with a "ph" or a "v"?"

"A 'ph' I think," he replied, so I signed his envelope.

This was the worst case by a couple of furlongs but there are two other witless fools wandering around England in the firm belief that, not only have they met Stephen Fry, but they have also acquired his autograph. I got a reply from one of the agencies saying that there was not so much demand for Stephen Frys but did I know any Gordon Browns?

What I really wanted was a job that paid well but gave me the freedom to come and go as I pleased. Quite by coincidence the following Thursday's *Daily Mail* seemed to have the answer. Amdega, the upmarket conservatory company, were advertising for new designers. My godmother Mo had an Amdega conservatory and I had always dreamed of working with the company; the idea of visiting rich people in their beautiful stately homes filled me with a sense of belonging. In the last seven years I had never seen Amdega in the *Daily Mail* Thursday job section. Was I finally about to be dealt a decent hand?

No. It was impossible. What did I know about design? Bugger all. I could not draw for toffee and why would Amdega even consider talking to a guy with my background? They would almost certainly want experienced designers, not foot-in-the door sales reps.

"Call them, you idiot." Kasia advised. I did and they asked me to send them a copy of my Curriculum Vitae. As expected I heard nothing.

Two months later I was just about to go to bed when the phone rang.

"Hello, can I speak to Rupert Miller please?"

"Speaking. Do you know what time it is?" I barked. "It is past 11:00pm and you have just woken my son. Thanks a bunch mate!"

"Oh I am terrible sorry. My name is Ian Mitchell, from Amdega. I'd like to meet you."

Amdega had been going since 1874 and surprisingly I was hired. Amdega was very much the 'Rolls-Royce' of the conservatory world, or so I was led to believe. My previous direct sales experience with Willowbrook was do the deal on the day or not at all. This was a very different kettle of fish. The sale process required two to four meetings, hours of drawing designs and probably lasted six to ten weeks so, for the first few months I was living off fresh air. To make matters worse, prospects were cancelling meetings once they had read the appalling reviews about Amdega. After much digging I found out that Amdega were in serious trouble and my dream of working for this paragon was completely shattered. In addition my sales 'patch' overlapped both the National Sale Manager's and the Area Sales Manager's so I was getting the crumbs from their tables.

After a miserable year I was 'let go' and found myself in nearly the same predicament as I had been on my return from

Poland. At least Kasia had a job but I needed to get back into something very quickly.

My good friend Martin Sunderland had followed me from Willowbrook to Amdega wearing the same rose-tinted spectacles that I had bought. He lasted less time than I did and was by now ensconced with a stair lift company. After a telephone call or two I joined him. It was, without doubt, the worst job I had ever had. In my desperation I had also taken out a deferred payment bank loan which now required servicing so I was back in the pickle factory. When in the fuck was my luck going to change or was I destined to join the ranks of terminal born losers?

While I was flogging over-priced stair lifts I kept my beady eye in permanent scan mode on the Thursday job section of the *Daily Mail*. Pride prevented me from scurrying back to Willowbrook and I'm glad it did as no sooner had I banished all these negative waves from my head, another golden goose arrived in the form of Apropos Tectonic. An Amdega clone, Apropos designed and built beautiful orangeries and conservatories, not in hardwood but aluminium. The big advantage, so they claimed, was aluminium required zero maintenance and, as they were now recruiting via the *Daily Mail* for designers in the North West, I was quite happy to believe anything.

I met Gary Shaw, the Apropos Regional Sales Manager, at the Chester Services on the M56 and was instantly given the North West of England and North Wales as my area. I was flooded with enquiries and with my recent Amdega training holding up well I made some swift sales. It was beginning to look like 2009 was going to be the start of something new.

No sooner had I started with Apropos I began to get very tired, probably due to the miles I was driving and the sheer number of meetings I was having. In my first three months I grossed over £30,000. It was like winning in Vegas but without the risk. Our new found wealth had enabled Kasia to scale down the teaching job and embark on a three year Fine Art degree at Glyndwr University. The only downer in our lives then was that Patryk's new orthopaedic surgeon, Mr Trivedi, had advised us that the first operation on Patryk's back had not been 100% successful and that he would require further surgery. However, it wasn't our son who was admitted to hospital next.

I was working my bollocks off and loving every minute of my new found triumph. In my enthusiasm for this new job, I disregarded the dizzy spells and pangs of thirst that were beginning to creep into my everyday life. One evening, on my way back from Manchester, I had to stop my car on the hard shoulder of the M62, get out and shake myself to clear my head. The next morning I felt so awful I went straight to the doctor who immediately pricked my finger, collected a drop of blood and tested it on a small handheld machine.

"You are going straight to hospital Mr. Miller." Dr. Cooper ordered.

"I can't. I'm driving to Poland for Christmas tomorrow."

"Mr. Miller, it's your decision but I think you are about to fall into a diabetic coma." Enough said.

So Type Two diabetes had come to the party and it was entirely self-inflicted as there was no record of it in my family. It looked like all those years of drinking and smoking had finally caught up with me. I'd stopped smoking years ago, but I still drank wine. This now also stopped.

After four days in hospital they managed to get my blood sugar levels under control and I was out just in time for Christmas. In the New Year I started on my new diet regime and medication plan which I'd now have to follow for the rest of my life. Fortunately, my new predicament had no effect on my business. In fact, since I was alcohol-free, I was considerably sharper and business positively blossomed.

Events in 2010 turned out even rosier after the enormous success of Patryk's latest and soon to be confirmed, final back operation; two titanium rods and twenty eight screws had done the trick. I ended 2010 as 'Top Designer' for Apropos Tectonic and Kasia was really enjoying her degree course. Life, once again, was sweet but this could surely only mean one thing. I continued to prosper at Apropos however, something was not right; so in the autumn of 2011 I started talking to a new company, David Salisbury Joinery Ltd, the acknowledged successor to Amdega, and by the end of 2011 Apropos Tectonic went into administration. To my surprise Apropos Conservatories Ltd. resurfaced from the ashes on the first of January 2012 but I had decided that I could no longer be involved with them. Since my move I have enjoyed far more success with David Salisbury than I could ever have anticipated.

Now as I write, Patryk is studying Psychology at university and we are very proud of him. After two major back surgeries and plenty of pain he has straightened nicely, and, as there is no prosthetic that would increase the dexterity of his right hand he has decided to live with it. He will, no doubt, deal with prejudice just as effectively as Julian did. He really is our '*brave little soldier*'.

Mrs. Miller, having gained a First Class Honours Degree in Fine Art and an MA in Art Practice, has just gone back into teaching with a view to putting her recently acquired new skills to good use. She will also, hopefully, be exhibiting at all the finest galleries around the globe.

After Patryk started at university we decided to have a clear out. In the cellar we found a cardboard box full of old videos, among them were Julian's campaign tapes and the documentary, *Week In Week Out*, made by Noreen Bray of BBC Wales. I took them all to Boots and had them converted to DVDs.

I had not been in touch with the Haemophilia Society since my brother died but continued to follow their progress with the Contaminated Blood Bill. It does not look like they are getting very far. Loads of letters lobbying MPs but no cash for the needy. Not really surprising as there are only around 6,000 haemophiliacs in the UK.

The haemophiliacs need for cash now mirrors the need I had to satiate my tuck cravings while at primary school. They cannot wait for government handouts or for some superstar to decide to sponsor their cause. Money is required now. Somehow I needed to devise a way of getting some cash quickly.

I was lying in my bath one evening and I thought, *what if I was to write a book about how my brother's death changed my life*? And how, sporadically having been able to pull the right rabbit out of the right hat at the right time, I have just about managed to stumble across the finishing line. The book would...

Note

Sadly, until everybody has, in some way, been touched by AIDS, then no number of government initiatives will succeed in educating people on the destructive power of this terrible disease. It is indiscriminate and will choose victims at random. In my brother's day, the saddest part was that the haemophiliacs had no choice regarding their blood for transfusion – they had to accept the risk of using the imported American blood. At the time, the Committee on Safety of Medicines were more frightened of running out of blood than they were of the damage infected blood might cause.

Now, almost 23 years since Julian died, and still the compensation battles continue against the government. Of the 1,200 haemophiliacs originally infected, over 800 have died. The remainder and the surviving families of the dead face daily financial hardship. Successive governments have totally missed the point. It *was the* government who perpetrated "*the worst treatment disaster in the history of the NHS...*" (Lord Robert Winston), and it *is the* government who have a moral responsibility to pay up, and pay up enough to allow victims to live; not just exist. It may still take years to get any compensation, so if you would like to help, then you can make a direct donation to the Haemophilia Society. www.haemophilia.org.uk

For donations to other countries societies please visit the respective websites.

8573687R00137

Printed in Great Britain
by Amazon.co.uk, Ltd.,
Marston Gate.